THREE MONTHS IN CASHMERE

Patrick Riches

THREE MONTHS IN CASHMERE

from a Lady's Diary,

May, June, July, 1887

By

Mary Elizabeth Sykes

Edited by

Patrick Pinches

Pearl Press

First published in Great Britain by Pearl Press

ISBN 978-0-9565001-9-9

Printed and bound by Good News, Ongar, England

Typeset by Yanina Goldenberg, Moscow

For Meg Chapman - without her foresight this book would have been stillborn.

And for her great-grandchildren.

My thanks to Judith, my wife, for her endless support, and to all at Pearl Press for their vision in publishing this Diary

CONTENTS

INTRODUCTION

'Oh! He's little but he's wise,
He's a terror for his size
And he does not advertise
Does our Sykes.'

'He has eyes all up his coat,
There's a bugle in his throat,
And you cannot play the goat
Under Sykes.'

'He's the Duke of 'Aggey-chal',
He's a bloke what's done us well,
And we'd follow him to 'ell,
Wouldn't we Sykes.'

******

The author and poet, Rudyard Kipling, wrote these words about Mr Thomas (Tom) Gaskell Sykes, who was the Principal of La Martiniere College in Lucknow, India, for over thirty years at the end of the 19th century. In his well-known book, *Kim*, Kipling also based the school attended by his character on La Martiniere.

My interest in both Tom Sykes and La Martiniere College was ignited by Mrs Meg Chapman, the granddaughter of Tom and, for the past forty-plus years, my mother-in-law. Some while ago, Meg realised that the three handwritten exercise books that she had inherited from Emily, Tom's daughter, were in danger of being unreadable if they were not somehow preserved, and she typed out the entire work. This text, written by Lizzie, Tom's wife, described a three-month trek through Kashmir undertaken by the two of them in 1887. Accompanying the text were about twenty sketches of places seen on this journey, drawn by Lizzie.

Much prose and poetry has been lavished on this exquisite fairyland, but few have been as evocative as that by one of the most famous of all Kashmiris, Jawaharlal Nehru, in his autobiography:

> *'Like some supremely beautiful woman, whose beauty is almost impersonal and above human desire, such was Kashmir in all its feminine beauty of river and valley and lake and graceful trees. And then another aspect of its magic beauty would come into view, a masculine one, of hard mountains and precipices, and snow-capped peaks and glaciers, and cruel and fierce torrents rushing down to the valleys below. It had a hundred faces and innumerable aspects, ever-changing, sometimes smiling, sometimes sad and full of sorrow……It was like the face of the beloved that one sees in a dream and that fades away on awakening…….'*

All of these aspects are described in Lizzie's own words in her diary.

Having ensured that the contents of this diary would be saved for future generations of the family, Meg and Judith, my wife, stowed them safely for several years. Just recently, two events have occurred that have renewed our interest in the diary – the ongoing political manoeuvrings to find a solution to the Kashmir problem, and the advances in digital technology that enable sketches to be easily reproduced and enhanced. We believed that the diary and the drawings, describing a part of British India one hundred and twenty years ago, might well be of interest to historians and Indo-philes alike.

I had recently completed writing my own memoirs, and so I decided to undertake the editing of the diary and sketches for publication, since they describe somewhere in the world that undoubtedly no longer exists as Lizzie saw it in 1887. In order to put the diary in context, I feel it necessary to provide some background information on Tom and Lizzie Sykes and their family, and on La Martiniere College, which was so central to their lives. Unfortunately, Meg died before I was able to complete the task that I had undertaken.

Patrick Pinches

August 2008

Thomas Gaskell and Mary Elizabeth Sykes in 1881 with Emily Sykes aged 3 and (centre) a niece

BACKGROUND

Thomas Gaskell Sykes (Tom) was born on 31st January 1844, the third of thirteen children born to Joseph and Mary (née Gaskell) Sykes. He graduated from London University with a BA and, after a few years teaching in England, sailed for India to take up an appointment as First Master at La Martiniere College, Lucknow, on 25th March 1871. After only three months he was promoted to Head Master on 14th June 1871, a position he held for nine years before his appointment as Principal, from 1st March 1880. He was Principal of La Martiniere until his retirement, aged 65, thirty years later – the longest serving Principal in the history of the College. He and his wife then returned to England and lived in Ealing, where Tom died on 6th December 1942, just missing the birth of his great-granddaughter, Judith (my wife), four months later.

Mary Elizabeth Sykes (née Burrows), known as Lizzie, the diarist of this trek in the Vale of Kashmir, was born on 31st December 1845. Her uncle, Sir J. Cordy Burrows, a prominent surgeon who lived in Brighton, was President of the Sacred Harmonic Society, which gave the first performance of *The Elijah* in London. The Burrows family came from Liss in Norfolk, and it was there that Lizzie married Tom on 2nd January 1873. They then sailed for India where, apart from very infrequent visits to England to see their children at boarding schools, they remained until 1909. Lizzie died in Ealing in 1928, fourteen years before her beloved husband, Tom.

Lizzie and Tom had six children during the first ten years of their married life, all except the sixth being born in Lucknow, and only one dying in infancy. Their fifth child was Maurice Gaskell Sykes, born on 10th December1879, my wife's grandfather. After school and university in England, Maurice joined the Indian Civil Service where he served as Assistant Collector of Taxes at Kistra from 1906, and then subsequently at Tinnevelly and at Penukonda Street. He married Constance Mary Lillian Roberts (known as Lillian) at Golders Green, London, on 4th September 1919, whilst serving as Judge/Magistrate in Chittoor district, Andrha Pradesh. Their first child was born there in June 1920 but unfortunately lived for only one hour. My mother-in-law, Mary Edith Gaskell (Meg) Sykes, was born at Chittoor on 23rd July 1921, and Lillian was then advised not to go through childbirth again. However, in 1925 she was again pregnant and, for the sake of her own and her unborn baby's health, the family moved back to England. These precautions were unfortunately to no avail – while giving birth to a stillborn son, Lillian sadly died in March 1926. Maurice was devastated by this double loss and immediately retired from the Indian Civil Service, eventually taking Holy Orders in the Church of England. Meg was raised by Maurice's sister, Emily, in Tom's home in Ealing.

Through one of those strange coincidences that happen in families, a school teacher named Jane Denize Callaway, from the Channel Isles, set sail for India in 1911 to take up a teaching post in Calcutta. There she met and married a poet/banker called John Alexander Chapman (JAC), then the Librarian of the Imperial Library, Calcutta. They had five children, the fourth of whom, Commander Paul Charles Chapman, DSO, OBE, DSC*, married Tom Sykes' granddaughter, Meg Sykes. The coincidence? – the school which Denize joined was La Martiniere Calcutta, a sister establishment of Tom's college at Lucknow.

A second strange coincidence in this family tale is that, like JAC, Lizzie Sykes was also a poet, although unlike him not a published one. The family unfortunately holds only one of her poems, which was written during the First World War as part of a series titled *Songs from a Captain.* Lizzie's second son, Oliver John Sykes, born in 1875, was Financial Adviser to the King of Siam until the outbreak of that war, when he joined the Heavy Artillery. He was killed in France in 1916. Whether Lizzie wrote the poems before or after his death is not known but, judging from the sadness of this poem, one can assume that he had already died:

WHEN I AM GONE

1

The sun will shine, the shadows fall,
The rain drips softly on and on,
The lark will sing, the cuckoo call
When I am gone.
The grass will wane, the flowerets blow,
The fruit will ripen in the sun,
Fair morns will smile, sweet sunsets glow,
When my sad day is done.

2

The memory, the thought of me,
A little while will linger on,
And then I shall forgotten be,
When I am gone.
But through my sleep, so still and deep,
When eyes are sealed, and lips are dumb,
A light may break and I shall wake
And know that morn hath come.

3

Oh dark, dread death we turn from thee
With helpless anguish, shrinking fears,
Oh Hope of Immortality,
We cling to thee with tears?
Oh dark dread death, thy icy breath
Brings helpless anguish, shrinking fears,
Oh Hope of Immortality
Thy dawning dries our tears!

JAC's first-born child, Patrick, joined the Royal Navy in 1932, and at the outbreak of the Second World War was serving in the submarine HMS Rainbow. While in the Mediterranean in October 1940 the 'Rainbow' simply disappeared with no survivors. To this day the cause of this disaster has not been firmly established but it is believed that the submarine, while submerged, was in collision with an Italian merchant ship. Patrick's younger brother Paul, my father-in-law, also served in submarines and had a very distinguished war record. Ironically, Patrick was born at the beginning of the First World War on 24th September 1914 and JAC, who was a peace-loving man, wrote a lengthy poem at his birth that almost foresees Patrick's death in war. In view of its length only a part of this poem is reproduced here, but the extracts chosen illustrate JAC's fears for his son's future:

TO P. C.

What do I wish for thee, my little one?
I wish thee all the common wish of men
For sons new-born – strength, joy, and length of days,
The love of many and the love of one.

These wish I for thee, little one, and more –
The things of the mind, knowledge of every kind,
To be drawn through every pore – fine sense made finer
By love of book-lore, music, statuary,
Painting and architecture – all good work
In wood, silk, ivory, metals, porcelain.
Be these thy love too, as they have been ours,

Thy Mother's and mine, first for their own delight,
Then as a link 'twixt us and other men,
Living and dead, English and alien.
Who are a man's friends?.........................

……………

I wish thee more, my little one. Thy birth,
Full in the sight of Himalayan snows,
Fell when the world was deeply stirred. Be that
A quickener in thee, but not to deeds
Dreadful as those that fill the world with awe
At so much strength, such grim tenacity,
Such toil, such skill – oh, but these words are weak!
My son, a little while ere thou wast born
In a small peaceful house that gentle birds
Pass in their summer, winter journeyings,
There broke upon the world such awful doom,
That if our faces should be turned to stone,
To sobs our voices, so that never more
Should laughter sound in any house of ours,
It were no marvel. But these winters past,
I pray God send His weeds to cover up
The fields of Europe. Peace to them and thee,
Peace all thy days to thee, and tasks of peace.

……………………….

So most I wish, my son, that thou mayest see
The beauty of the ways of manly men,

And seeing follow. Be God's gift to thee
(This day thou art His gift to us) the strength
That makes men brave, just, truthful, noble, pure,
Courteous and gentle, kind, magnanimous,
Reverent of women, tender, patient, good,
And faithful. ………………

………………………………………………

All these be thine, joined with the touch divine,
The something, none knows what, that keeps the spring
Of life a pure, sweet holy, radiant thing.

To return to Lizzie and Tom, in 1887 Tom decided that he would like to make a three-month trek of the Vale of Kashmir. Not wishing to miss out on the adventure (and also, possibly more accurately, not wishing to let Tom off on his own for three months!), Lizzie accompanied him. Fortunately, she not only kept a detailed diary of their journey but also sketched places and things that interested her en route. These sketches have, fortuitously, survived the passing of the years, and are reproduced here with the diary.

There is always a problem in transcribing Indian place names into English, and the spellings used by Lizzie were not always consistent. Therefore, throughout the diary, I have used the spellings to be found in the 15th Edition of *The Tourist's Guide to Kashmir, Ladakh, Skardo, etc*, edited by Major Arthur Neve. However, throughout her Diary Lizzie used 'Cashmere', rather than 'Kashmir', and I have retained this usage since the journey there was her dream. I have also included a Glossary of the local words used by her in the narrative.

LA MARTINIERE COLLEGE

Major-General Claud Martin was born in Lyon, France, on 4th January 1735. In 1751 he signed on as a private soldier with the Compagnie des Indes Orientales, (the French equivalent of the Honourable East India Company) and arrived in Pondicherry, India, on 20th July 1752. He did not leave India for the next fifty years, dying there on 13th September 1800. By 1761 France's dreams of a French Empire in India had ended, and Martin was appointed to the Honourable East India Company's army in September 1763, becoming a most successful 'soldier of fortune' with the British. He served actively with the Company until October 1779 reaching the rank of Major, when he became an adviser to the Nawab-Wazir of Oudh in Lucknow. In this capacity he acted as a link between the Company and the Nawab in the latter's dealings with the British. He was trustworthy and influential with both the Court of Oudh and the Board of Directors of the Honourable East India Company, and he became extremely rich. He was also very active in the Company's army again in the 1790's and was promoted to Major-General.

In his Will, which was a long and complicated one that took nearly forty years to settle, General Martin left an enormous sum of money for the endowment of three Colleges – one in his home town of Lyon in France, one in Calcutta, and one in Lucknow. The latter college was established in a grand house that Martin started to build in 1794 called 'Constantia' - the architecture of this building is extraordinarily ornate and, to this day, is regarded as a 'must see' for visitors to Lucknow. The College opened its doors to students in 1845, making it one of the older educational establishments in India, and its students came from both European and Indian (or 'Native' as General Martin's endowment referred to them) families. Twelve years later, by which time there were 267 pupils at the College,

Lucknow was embroiled in the Indian Mutiny. From June to November 1857 the British Residency was besieged by mutineers from the army of the Honourable East India Company, an event that has a firm place in the history books. Most of the boys were evacuated from the College but the staff and 67 of the boys moved into the Residency. Here they bravely played their parts in the siege, bearing arms with the soldiers, carrying ammunition, serving those besieged as hospital attendants, carrying messages, doing domestic duties in place of the servants who had absconded, and grinding wheat and corn – all in addition to their school studies. All but two of the boys lived through the siege. Years later the vital part played by the College was recognised by the British Government bestowing on La Martiniere College the right to carry a 'Flag' on ceremonial occasions – this is generally taken to be the equivalent of awarding the college Battle Honours, an honour which is unique outside Regiments in the British Army.

La Martiniere College grew over the years, its senior boys frequently gaining the top positions for entrance into Roorkee Educational College. Rudyard Kipling used the college as his inspiration for the school which Kim attended, and the college was subsequently used as a film set for the film *Kim*, starring Errol Flynn. Today, La Martiniere College boasts about 1700 pupils.

La Martiniere College

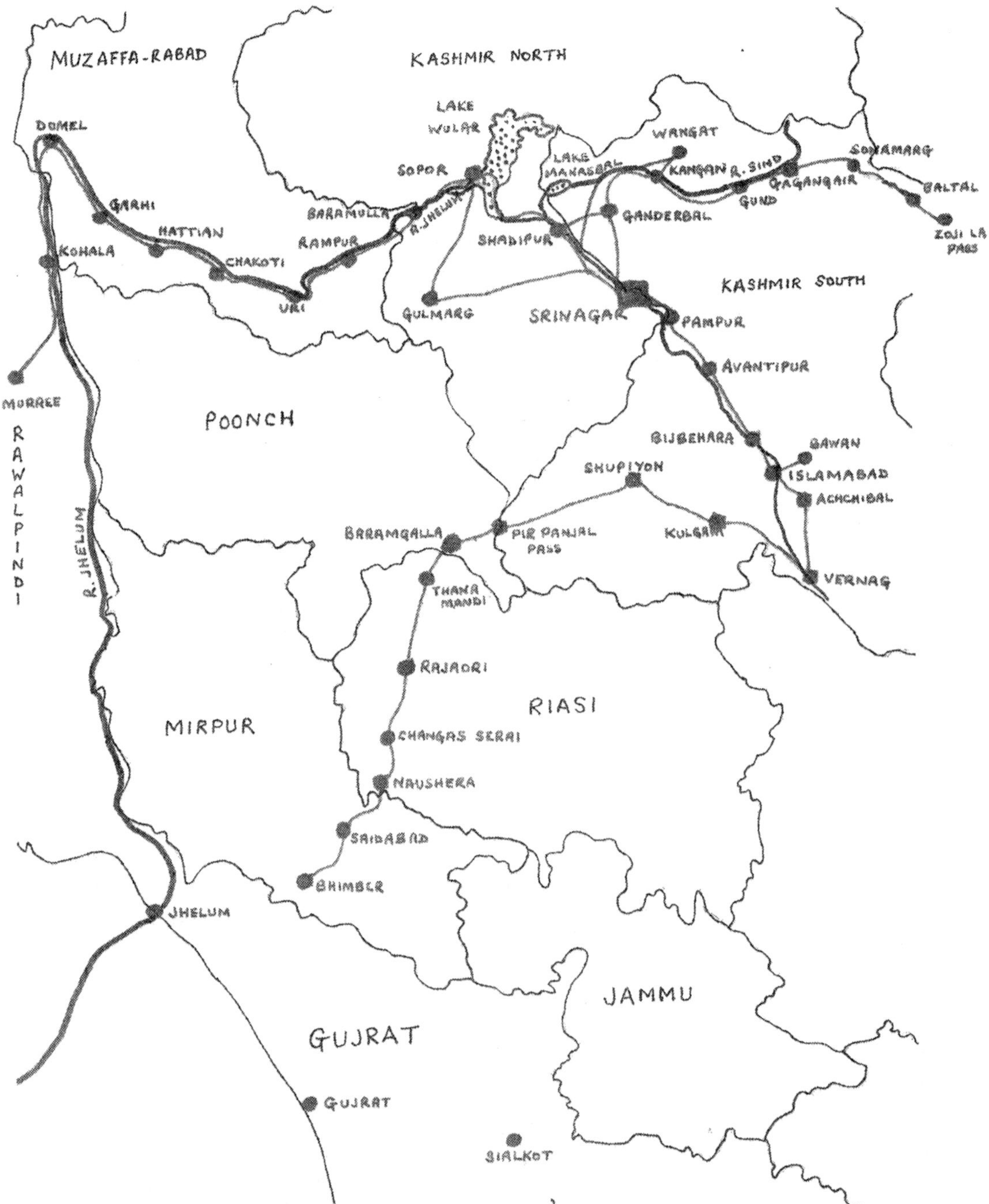

SYKES' ROUTE
May - July 1887.

SYKES' ROUTE

Place	Date Arrived (presumed)	Distance (miles)
Lucknow	.... 1st May (departed)	
Murree	.... 3rd May	.... (Rail)
Dewal	.... 9th May	 10
Kohala	.... 9th May	 10
Domel	.... 10th May	 20
Garhi	.... 10th May	 16
Hattian	.... 10th May	 10
Chakoti	.... 11th May	 16
Uri	.... 12th May	 18
Rampur	.... 13th May	 14
Baramulla	.... 14th May	 10
Sopor	.... 14th May	.... (Boat)
Wular Lake	.... 15th May	.... (Boat)
Shadipur	.... 15th May	.... (Boat)
Srinagar	.... 16th May	.... (Boat)
Dal Lake	.... 26th May	.... (Boat)
Shalimar Gardens	.... 26th May	.... (Boat)
Lake Manasbal	.... 6th June	.... (Boat)
Ganderbal	.... 8th June	.... (Boat)
Larri	.... 9th June	 2
Wangat	.... 12th June	 13
Kangan	.... 14th June	 10
Gund	.... 15th June	 14
Gagangair	.... 16th June	 9
Sonamarg	.... 17th June	 10
Baltal	.... 18th June	 7
Zoji La Pass	.... 18th June	 7
Sonamarg	.... 18th June	 14
Gagangair	.... 19th June	 10
Gund	.... 20th June	 9

Kangan	.... 21st June	 14
Ganderbal	.... 22nd June	 10
Shadipur	.... 23rd June	.... (Boat)
Srinagar	.... 23rd June	.... (Boat)
Sopor	.... 24th June	.... (Boat)
Babamarishi	.... 25th June	 22
Gulmarg	.... 26th June	 5
Srinagar	.... 27th June	 27
Pampur	.... 3rd July	.... (Boat)
Avantipur	.... 4th July	.... (Boat)
Sorsoo	.... 4th July	.... (Boat)
Bijbehara	.... 5th July	.... (Boat)
Khanabal	.... 5th July	.... (Boat)
Islamabad	.... 6th July	 1
Bawan	.... 7th July	 6
Martand	.... 8th July	 3
Achchibal	.... 8th July	 3
Vernag	.... 9th July	 16
Kulgam	.... 12th July	 14
Shupiyon	.... 13th July	 18
Hirpur	.... 14th July	 8
Aliabad Serai	.... 15th July	 13
Pir Panjal Pass	.... 16th July	 3
Poshiana	.... 16th July	 8
Baramgalla	.... 16th July	 10
Thana Mandi	.... 20th July	 10
Rajaori	.... 21st July	 14
Changas Serai	.... 22nd July	 15
Naushera	.... 23rd July	 11
Saidabad	.... 24th July	 10
Bhimber	.... 25th July	 15
Lucknow	.... 29th July	.... (Rail)
	Total	485 Walk/Ride

GLOSSARY

Local Word	Meaning
Anail- nag	Sulphur spring
Baksheesh	Tip/gratuity
Bawarchi	Cook
Bawarchikhana	Cookhouse
Bhisti	Water carrier/supplier
Caravanserai	Rest-house
Charpoy	Light bedstead
Chick	Grass blind/screen
Chillumchee	Wash basin, of brass or tinned copper
Chittie	Written note/testimonial
Chota haziri	Light, early breakfast
Chowkidar	Watchman
Chula	Fireplace, made of mud
Chupattis	Small, flat, thin cakes of coarse unleavened bread
Dhobie	Washerman/washerwoman
Dhurrie	Heavy cotton floor cloth/carpet
Dustoori	Customary fee/commission

Kangri	Small wicker-covered pot, filled with glowing charcoal
Khansama	House steward and butler
Khud	Precipice/deep ravine/chasm
Kilta	Basket covered with leather
Kotwal	Chief police officer/magistrate
Morghie	Chicken
Mussack	Leather water-bag/inflated skin
Nautch	Performance of traditional dance by professional dancing girls
Numdah	Rug/carpet of coarse wool
Puttoo	Coarse cloth, made of the hair of the Kashmir goat
Sepoy	Soldier
Seraglio	Harem
Sola topi	Pith helmet
Syce	Groom
Tekadar	Man in charge
Tiffin	Light meal/luncheon
Tonga	Two-wheeled cart
Zenana	Women's apartments

CHAPTER 1

'Who has not heard of the Vale of Cashmere,
With its roses the brightest that earth ever gave,
Its temples and grottoes and fountains as clear
As the love- lighted eyes that hang o'er their wave?'

We had not only heard of it but it was the 'dream of our life' to visit the Happy Valley; and, as we lived in India within easy reach, we determined to realize our dream. As my husband found that he had three months' leave privilege due to him our object was to spend these three months in Cashmere with as much pleasure and as little expense as possible, for like the spouse of John Gilpin under similar circumstances,

'Though on pleasure I was bent
I had a frugal mind'

We resolved at the outset that the total cost of the tour from leaving home to returning to it should not exceed £100; whether this resolve was successfully carried out or not will appear in the sequel. *(Ed. – Not written or, if it were, it has been lost.)* Meanwhile, keeping this end in view, we gaily set about making arrangements.

The great thing seemed to be to have all the necessaries of life with as many of its comforts as possible, and at the same time to make our baggage light and compact. We had a Swiss Cottage tent weighing 130 lbs and two single-poled tents weighing 60 lbs each. When all our heavy luggage was packed comprising the above tents, camp-beds, tables, carpets, chairs, cooking pots, table requisites, saddles, baths etc., it weighed about 6 hundredweight. This we dispatched by rail a fortnight before we had to leave, hoping that on our arrival at Murree, the Indian Hill Station from which our march into Cashmere was to begin, we should find it there. When the time came for us to start, our personal baggage, with that of the servants we took with us, amounted to about 3 hundredweight more, so that altogether we had 9 hundredweight to carry about with us in Cashmere.

We could not get ready-made kiltas *(baskets covered with leather)* in our part of the world and, as they are at the same time both light and strong, they were more suitable for our purpose than trunks or boxes. So we got a man from the village who could make coolie baskets to come and work under our directions in the veranda. He speedily made some strong barrel-shaped baskets with lids,which were covered with skins by another of our villagers and, when furnished with chains and padlocks, these were our kiltas. Our bedding was wrapped up in a waterproof sheet as a protection against the rain, and after a few other preparations we were ready to start.

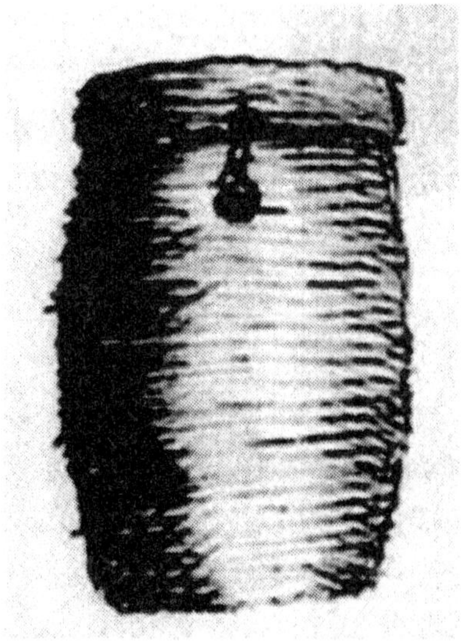

Sykes Kilta

We had a hot and weary railway journey of 800 miles which occupied two days and two nights, followed by 40 miles over rough roads in a country cart which brought us to Murree, 7500 feet up in the Himalayas where the cool and bracing air was much appreciated by us after the intense heat of the plains. The scenery too was beautiful, the snowy range being distinctly visible beyond the intervening mountains.

View of the snows, Murree

Our heavy baggage, alas, had not yet arrived, so we made a virtue of necessity and spent a pleasant week drinking in the sweet pure air, feasting our eyes on the snowy range, and paying several visits daily to the office of the Phoenix Company, whose attractive advertisement in the 'Pioneer' had induced us to trust our baggage to them. Our constant visits and our clamour, now wheedling, now threatening, but always determined, had such an effect on them that at last they did something and our things arrived.

We promptly dispatched everything to Garhi a day or two in advance so as to be ready for us, and we ourselves started early in the morning of 9th May with high hopes and aspirations for our journey into Cashmere. Our intention had been to set off at 6 a.m. but as usual many things had to be done at the last moment and, through a misunderstanding, we had unfortunately sent off all our servants in advance with the greater part of the luggage. Owing to the stupidity of the man who loaded our few remaining effects on a mule, the ropes gave way just as we were starting and the whole burden fell to the ground in different directions. When this mishap had been remedied we made another attempt, I on a weak hill pony, and Tom on foot. The pleasure of the first stage was to a great extent spoilt by the mule, which turned out to be very sluggish and, as we had none of our servants with us, we felt bound to remain near it, and not to let it lag behind lest we should never see it again.

Our way lay gently downhill, and we went on quietly feasting our eyes on the most lovely mountain scenery till we had finished our first march of ten miles and arrived about noon at the rest-house at Dewal. This was a bare barn-like building; the furniture too was very meagre. There were, however, two chairs and a table which was all that was immediately required.

After unpacking our provisions and taking a refreshing meal I lay down on a not very tempting looking charpoy *(light bedstead)* and had a nap while Tom smoked in the veranda. At about 4 p.m. we set off for another march of 10 miles and as I had not been on horseback for some years, I thought it rather a feat to attempt more than twenty miles in one day.

The road now began to descend rapidly so that I soon got very tired of riding continually downhill, all the more so as, Tom having gone on in front, my sole attendant was a small boy of twelve. On my asking him if he could alter my saddle which had slipped forward and was extremely uncomfortable, he sadly confessed himself unable to do so and I had to go on as best I could till at last, coming up with a coolie carrying some of my luggage, I alighted, had the saddle rearranged and went on more comfortably. The path still continuing very steep in its descent, I looked in vain for a piece of level or rising ground to relieve the strain on the muscles of my back and feet, and began to think that

that favourite illustration of moralists, 'facilis descensus', was not quite perfect, or must be taken with a good deal of mental reservation, so by no means universal in its application. The way lay along the sides of the mountains following the course of the river Jhelum, which 'hastens along, conflicting and strong' at the bottom of a very deep and narrow valley that it must have carved out for itself in the course of ages.

At about sunset we reached the next stage, Kohala, where the rest-house on the bank of the river is fairly comfortable but, as it is shut in by lofty hills, not a breath of air was stirring and it was very hot. Whilst our dinner was being cooked we sat in the veranda and watched the lights appearing in a little village of flat-roofed huts on the opposite bank. They looked very near to us, but the noisy impetuous Jhelum rolled between. I never heard such a demonstrative river; its murmur filled the air. Just here it is very turbid and is covered with white wavelets all curving backwards from its breathless hurry.

At dinner the khansama's *(house steward)* son, a small but important little fellow, waited on us. He adopted all the airs of an experienced servant and spoke in a very loud voice, enumerating glibly the various delicacies within our reach. We found it quite impossible to sleep on account of the heat; I was overtired too. My nerves had not grown accustomed to mountain travelling so that I was continually imagining myself falling over hideous precipices, and I was quite glad to see the dawn,

At six o' clock we had chota haziri *(early breakfast)*, a snack which Anglo-Indians indulge in before the real breakfast, and after crossing the Jhelum by a fine suspension bridge, evidently the work of English engineers, we started in the tonga for Garhi. A tonga is a strongly built two-wheeled cart drawn by ponies; it holds three passengers besides the driver and the man who acts as syce *(groom)*; this last-named worthy perches on behind when not otherwise engaged, but at the least difficulty he rushes to the front encouraging the ponies with the most terrific shouts and yells as he runs by their side, or sits on the shaft and plies the whip with great energy and skill. The road, which follows the course of the river, is reasonably wide, but frightfully rough in places. The big boulders of which it is composed are only lightly covered with earth, and as this gets trodden down they speedily become apparent to more senses than one. The ponies were kept at a gallop all the way and as we banged and bumped along the result was sometimes most surprising. We held on with silent determination but sometimes an unusually emphatic bump would draw from us an audible groan. I have always thoroughly approved of that beautiful advice of Wordsworth's,

'never to blend my pleasure or my pain, with sorrow of the meanest thing that breathes'

but I soon became convinced that my pleasure in the beautiful scenery through which we were passing would be blended with a considerable amount of sorrow for the poor animals that conveyed me. I tried to think that this was only a passing time of tribulation as they probably rested all the winter but their dejected, hopeless appearance made my heart ache. They looked pretty well fed, however, and they are changed every six miles so their trials though tough are short and sharp.

After going at full speed for about twenty miles we came to Domel where there is a most delightful dak bungalow or posting rest-house - recently built by the Maharaja of Cashmere and really quite a model - on the banks of the river. We rested here for an hour and then, though it began to be very hot, we proceeded on our journey in the tonga. Various small catastrophes enlivened the way. At one place, as we were crossing a bridge without any parapet, notwithstanding our driver's alarming horn we ran foul of a herd of cattle. One unfortunate cow fell down in trying to get out of our way, and our wheels nearly went over it as it lay with its head hanging over the bridge. As soon as we backed to let it get up it tried to jump into the water and was only prevented by its owner hanging on to its tail, shouting lustily. As we passed on we looked back and saw it was running about, apparently not much the worse for its fright.

The last ten miles of the stage from Domel to Garhi were very rough and trying. In one place, for instance, we had just passed carefully over a bridge labeled 'unsafe' when one of the ponies put his hoof into a hole on the road and fell heavily, which necessitated our alighting and waiting in the shade while our men extricated the poor creature. Both its knees were badly cut, but the syce washed the places at a little spring hard by, plastered some earth over them, and then coolly proceeded to harness it to the cart again. We wanted to walk but the heat was dreadful and we were some miles from the changing place, so with much compunction we got in again and off we galloped as furiously as ever. I tried to think that perhaps it hurt the poor creature less to gallop than to go slowly, but am afraid there was no foundation for the hope.

After doing 36 miles in the tonga we arrived very tired at Garhi. The bungalow was a mere shed, and even such as it was it was full. The dak bungalow chowkidar *(watchman)* offered us one room like a cattle shed which we refused to enter, and having at this point come up with our servants and baggage, we pitched a tent on the bank of the river and had tiffin *(luncheon)*. The dry air of these parts seems to make us very thirsty, and as the water was not cool enough to drink with pleasure, we made some hot tea, which is soothing and suitable under all circumstances. After unpacking our kiltas and changing our clothes so as to be able to ride the following stages, we sent off as many coolies as we could get, and started for Hattian, some ten miles off where we hoped we should find a comfortable bungalow for the night. Unfortunately, we could not get enough coolies and some of our packages had to be left behind.

While Tom was seeing about these I mounted my horse and rode forward. This good strong horse was one which had been sent down all the way from Srinagar to Murree to await us by that excellent man Pandit Janki Pershad, the Governor of Cashmere, to whom we had an introduction. Hitherto we had not been able to use it as our saddles were behind with the heavy luggage but now, with a strong steady horse and my own saddle, I found riding a very different thing from what I had experienced the previous day. I soon came up with our well-laden coolies who informed me, in moving strains, that they should die of their loads. I reassured them with cheerful confidence on this point and moved on, feeling thankful that it did not fall to my lot to have to carry the said loads. The road was now nothing but a rocky path winding through a wild and mountainous region. My horse crawled with me down places like a flights of stairs, and up rocks which I should have hesitated to climb. He walked steadily along the edges of precipices and won my unchanging respect by the gravity with which he contemplated, and the delicate way in which he finally walked over, a rickety bridge that came in our path. I felt that a horse of such sagacity and deliberation would not be likely to go over the khud *(precipice)* if he could help it, and that all I had to do, therefore, was to sit still and remotely direct operations.

I have always known that the scenery of the Himalayas was on a most grand and magnificent scale, but its vastness far surpassed all that I had ever imagined. As the road winds along, the mighty hills open out in combinations of ever increasing beauty, but there were some terrible places to pass over and I could sometimes hear great boulders rolling and falling into the abyss beneath, giving me vivid and thrilling unpleasant reminders of what would be the consequences if my horse made a false step. Sometimes the road wound round the shoulder of a great mountain and, as we came to the turning point, first my horse's head would project over the edge and then his tail, and I felt that there was nothing to be done but to sit straight in the saddle and hope for the best. It was really terrible at times and I wondered that I was not more alarmed.

Soon darkness came on and I began to feel rather anxious about my husband whom I had not seen since starting as he had stayed behind to get off the luggage and had intended to follow on foot, but I trusted he was with some of the coolies who knew the road. The syce in charge of my horse assured me that the rest-house was on the side of the opposite hill and would in daylight be visible from the spot on which we then were. There were no lights in the direction in which he pointed and this did not look promising. After a steep descent into the valley we came to a bridge over which the syce went but which he pronounced unsafe for the horse. However, he said the stream was not wide and the horse would find his way across, so as it was too dark to see either bridge or stream I allowed the animal to take his own way. After a good deal of scrambling over stones, I found we were floundering in the water, whereupon I tucked up my feet as much as possible and after a few minutes of painful uncertainty we seemed to be on dry land again. Another steep ascent and we were at the rest-house, but darkness and silence reigned. The syce shouted and I too lifted up my voice with a will, and at last sleepy voices answered, and dim forms began to move on the roof of a hut hard by, where people appeared to be sleeping. Then a tiny glowworm of light came twinkling down the hillside, and an old man appeared who told me that there were no servants whatever belonging to the rest-house, and that there was nothing to be had at that time of night. I begged him to give me a light and after a long delay he brought a little earthen saucer with a wick and some oil. By its flickering light I perceived a table in the verandah, and a bottle with a candle stuck in it. Rejoicing at this find I ordered the candle to be lighted, but the man informed me that it belonged to a sahib *(English/European gentleman)*, and at the same moment I perceived dimly, coming through the darkness, the form of an English gentleman. He turned out to be a young doctor, a traveller like ourselves, who had lately come out from England and, as he did not know the language, my shouts and vociferations which had all been couched in excellent Hindustani, gave him no idea that I was an English lady till the light in the saucer revealed me, when he at once came forward and did the honours of the place.

He informed mc that the dak bungalow was a most wretched hole with scarcely any furniture; the floors were of mud and the walls tumbledown and dirty. He, however, was hospitable and gave me some water to drink and the only unbroken chair the house contained. He also attempted to light the candle in the bottle, but the wind promptly blew it out. My saucer lamp also having expired, we sat and conversed amicably in the dark. Our conversation was not very brilliant, for it is talking under difficulties, as Charles Lamb says,

'when you have to feel for the responsive smile on the face on your companion'.

Presently, loud shouts announced my husband's arrival; he had found the road very dangerous and had lost his way in the dark, but he seemed cheery and was certainly very hungry. I introduced my two friends and have no doubt they instinctively bowed their best, but they might as well have been making grimaces at each other in the dark - no-one would have been a bit the wiser.

As the servants had not yet appeared and there was nothing to eat we again called up the old tekadar *(man in charge)* and impressed upon him our hungry and forlorn condition, suggesting that he could at least give us some milk. He looked as if he thought it no joke to catch cows and goats for milking purposes in that wild hill country in the middle of the night. Being moved, however, by our hungry clamour and still more by the magic charm of baksheesh *(tip/gratuity)*, he promised to bring us something if we could wait an hour. At the end of the time he reappeared with a big bowl of milk and some chupatties and hard-boiled eggs which he had cooked. By this time too our servants began to straggle in looking very tired and dejected, and I soon fished from the depths of the tiffin basket a tin of a soup which was warmed in five minutes, and so we satisfied our longing souls. But when we wanted our beds to be unpacked and arranged, everybody seemed too jaded to remember where they were or how to put them together and, as there was a dilapidated old charpoy such as natives use in one of the rooms, I resolved to demean myself so far as to sleep on that - a decision I deeply regretted. As for my husband, he spread a dhurrie *(heavy cotton floor cloth)* in the veranda beside my charpoy, and having quite by accident lighted on his mattress and pillow, made himself comfortable.

There was a most suggestive looking hole in the mud floor near his feet which looked as if it might have been a cockatrice's den or a snake hole at the very least. One of the servants stuffed it up with a bundle of string in a very perfunctory manner, but this did not prevent his mind running on rats and snakes all night long, and whenever I moved and thus made my crazy old bed creak he made a hissing noise in his sleep to scare away the supposed enemies. The night was hot and close, we were down in a hollow quite surrounded by mountains and I lay awake watching the coolies and servants clustering around a fire of sticks, cooking their simple food. At last they all subsided and then the moon rose and glorified the scene. At dawn I rose and dragged my bed inside the house in consideration for the feelings of our fellow traveller so that he might not be scandalized when he came out of his stifling room in which, I am grieved to say, he had locked himself up out of similar feelings of consideration for me.

The coolies soon began to be very busy again cooking chupattis *(small, flat thin cakes of coarse unleavened bread)*, their principal food during the day. Some of them were wearing curious shoes of coarse grass which they wear tied on their feet like sandals to protect them from the stones and to help them to climb. Most English travellers follow their example when they leave the beaten tracks, as these grass shoes are said to prevent your slipping both on grass and on the snow. I tried them once or twice but they hurt me and were altogether most uncomfortable, and as I had good strong comfortable boots of unblacked leather I never felt the want of them though I had a great deal of climbing to do before my travels were finished. The coolies are strong good-natured creatures, clad in garments of dirty drab puttoo *(coarse cloth made of the hair of the Cashmere goat)*. Sometimes they accumulate all their clothes in a lump on that part of their person where their burden presses most, but generally they allow their drapery to hang about in the most astonishing manner. I noticed some queer little arrangements like the bodies of dead animals on the top of their loads, and upon enquiry found that they were skins containing their private property such as grain for food. One had a pretty brown kidskin, and another a white Astrachan lambskin.

Grass shoe

We did not start till 8 o'clock though we had a long march of sixteen miles before us, but stayed to get a substantial breakfast which was very necessary after our scanty dinner the night before. The old tekadar let Tom, my husband, have a nice strong pony, but without shoes, and we started gaily with a freshness in the air which made us enjoy every mile of our march. Besides the grand beauty of the distant scenery, our immediate surroundings were inexpressibly lovely, the oleanders and pomegranates, jasmines and other flowering shrubs, being all in bloom.

We had not gone far before we came up with a large drove of camels; there were two or three score of them. The path was too narrow for us to pass them, and as they came 'between the wind and our nobility' it was very disagreeable to have to follow them, so we took a terrific short cut up a place like the wall of a house and thus managed to get before them. But not long after, just as we were turning a sharp corner towards the end of a steep descent, we met a drove of heavily laden mules. It was impossible to pass them and there was no room even for the mules to turn back. I was nearly slipping over my horse's head at the time and he could not stir a step, so there was nothing for it but to dismount and, the mules being pushed flat against the side of the rock by their drivers, we crawled warily along the broken edge of the cliff holding on by the harness of the mules, one after the other, till we had passed the whole drove. The precipice below us went sheer down 1000 feet, and the Jhelum roared at the bottom, but strange to say I hardly thought of this but was only afraid of a kick from one of the beasts. The road runs the whole way along the side of the mountains at a great height, rarely less than that I have just mentioned, above the river. At one place we saw a very primitive bridge. It could not have been simpler, as it consisted of a single rope fastened to supports on either bank - it was lower on one side than on the other and the rope thus formed an inclined plane. We stopped to watch a man going across. From the distance at which we were above him, he seemed to sit on a small piece of wood suspended from the rope and, by pulling along the rope, to work himself gradually down the incline. The river was boiling beneath him, but he did not seem to be at all impressed by his situation and reached the other side in safety looking as if this perilous journey was quite an every day occurrence.

Soon after this we came to a lovely little mountain stream all fringed with maidenhead fern, where we alighted to let our horses drink, and we ourselves also could not resist the temptation, though not being au fait at drinking from mountain streams we got terribly splashed in the process.

At the end of about ten miles we came to a sort of rest-house for the horses and, while they were taking their ease, we climbed the hill to a delightful spot where there was a miniature waterfall. Its little airs and graces were delicious, its tiny splashes and gentle roars reminded us of a kitten playing at being a tiger. There were stones near this ambitious cascade tempting us to sit down, and over all was a huge tree, the first of the magnificent chenars *(oriental plane trees)* for which the Happy Valley is famous, whose branches fell round us like an arbour. So we rested and ate and drank; the cold morghie *(chicken)* was ambrosia and the milk which a man brought was nectar as we gazed entranced through our leafy veil at the golden glories of the Himalayan scenery beyond. I found it hard work to get down from this shady perch and could scarcely manage it even with the help of a stick, for I was not yet accustomed to mountain climbing. But we soon mounted our horses and after a couple of hours more were at our journey's end - Chakoti.

The servants had not arrived but we sat in the veranda and drank milk cheeringly and uncomplainingly. Privations were still new to us and at present were rather amusing than otherwise. The rest-house was the usual dirty dilapidated barn but it was very prettily situated and a little noisy stream came rushing down from the mountain behind and ran chattering past our door. We whiled away the time by dropping our handkerchiefs in at the top of the stream and catching them at the bottom; but in time even this excitement palled and with the weariness of hope deferred we climbed a hill which commanded the road by which our belongings might be expected. Presently, to our great joy, round a distant bend in the road appeared the figure of our sturdy old bawarchi *(cook)*, and close behind him came a coolie laden with a basket wherein our hopes of a meal were centered. We greeted them with a shout of unfeigned delight and ran down the hill in a most unseemly hurry so as to be ready, though our reason told us that we should have to wait at least an hour before anything could be prepared.

We had had a hot ride from Hattian and, there being but little shade on the road, I was terribly sunburnt, my nose in fact, which being slightly retroussé protrudes beyond the brim of my hat, was burnt to a fire red brown colour. Tom, with that want of consideration peculiar, I believe, to husbands, did not fail to remark on this. His nose, being decidedly Roman, had not suffered but I was able to retort by making withering remarks upon the bristly condition of his chin, which brought him into his usual state of deferential submission. I have observed that a man who has not shaved for three or four days is easily suppressed and made to feel small. When the condition has lasted a week or so he is accustomed to the figure he cuts and, becoming bold and brazen, is not so amenable.

The remainder of the day we spent quietly at Chakoti resting after all our fatigues. There was a group of native huts and shops just outside the compound, the flat roofs of which seemed to be a playground for children and a grazing ground for goats. These flat roofed huts which seem to prevail in these parts are simply built of pine trunks against the side of a hill, which forms the back and often sometimes the sides of the building; earth is beaten down firmly over the roof which is very soon covered with a crop of weeds and waving grass which gives the houses the comical look of being decorated with a thick head of hair.

Flat-roofed hut

The Cashmere goats are very handsome creatures. There is not much beauty in an ordinary goat; it has no curves and is all unexpected angles. On the other hand, the beautiful long silky hair of the animals we see here somewhat conceals their angularity and makes them look very elegant and graceful. They are of various colours, principally exquisite 'confections' of black and white, but the prettiest are of a delicate silver grey and a pale cream tan colour, shaded to brown.

We spent a restful day, after all our recent activity. The rooms of the bungalow of this place were so stuffy and dirty that we could only sit with comfort in the veranda. When dinner time came, finding that our lamp was not unpacked, we set about arranging the not quite original idea of a candle in a bottle, which was the only one that presented itself for our illumination but, alas, where was the bottle? We actually had not one empty. This looks as if we were teetotalers, but candour reluctantly obliges me to confess that we carried with us a keg of whisky with a tap to it which was as the apple of our eye and from which we drew enough to cheer but not to inebriate when 'so disposed'. Having therefore no bottle we fixed our candle by the primitive method of sticking it in its own grease on the table ourselves and the wind promptly blew it out. We barricaded it with all the means at our disposal but the wind was still too much for us and we had to resign ourselves to eat our dinner as best we could in the dark. Fortunately, however, at this auspicious moment the coolies lighted their cooking fire and by its fitful gleams we were enabled to find the way to our mouths. Our dinner nevertheless was as a matter of course a series of surprises; we got bones where we expected meat, lumps of fat where we hoped for potato, and sometimes it seemed that we had taken up all our mustard or salt at one fell swoop. We soon retired to rest having, with our usual consideration for our tired servants, decided not to unpack our own beds, as there were two decent looking charpoys in the house. Alas, we soon deeply regretted that we had been beguiled into sleeping on them, for all night long we were the prey of fleas and other ravenous animals. Sleep was impossible under these conditions and as the hours rolled slowly by we feebly and sleepily wished ourselves at home.

Before dawn we heard the coolies shouldering their burdens and starting so as to reach Uri, the next stage 18 miles off, before we came up with them. We ourselves started about seven. The way was as rough and picturesque as ever; it wound up and down, in and out, now descending quite into the valley to cross a stream, and now giving us a cruel climb to regain our lost elevation. My horse addressed himself with such sturdy valour to climb the steep ascents that I named him 'Greatheart' on the spot. His demeanour inspired me with great confidence and, having now become accustomed to the tremendous precipices and chasms on every hand, I gave myself up to the enjoyment of the wealth of the beauty around me.

The road was deliciously shady; now and then we got glorious views of the distant snow-clad peaks. The trees and flowering shrubs grew more and more beautiful and luxuriant. The oleanders with their bunches of pink blossom, which surrounded us at first, had now disappeared and today the pomegranate with its brilliant scarlet blossom is everywhere mingled with huge bushes of wild roses. The flowers are white and in great profusion, and if I were an Italian I should please myself by thinking that nature in these parts had donned my colours for the time being. Besides these, shrubs of white and yellow jasmine scented the air and there were many other flowers not so familiar to me. Maidenhair fern is a perfect weed, every little mountain stream is fringed with it. Indeed there is such profusion of loveliness around us, and such a setting of mountains and sky, as I never imagined in my wildest dreams. This country must be the despair of an artist as mere paint and canvas can never be made to represent the transparent violet pellucid beauty of its atmosphere, the vivid hues of its trees and flowers and the ethereal tints of its sky and water. And as to picturesque bits – why, it is one picturesque whole. It is a feast of form as well as of colour; every stone wears its drapery of moss and ferns with a native grace, and tempts you to sketch it.

As the way was long we rested now and then in some shady place by one of the little streamlets which everywhere come rushing down the mountain sides in eager haste to join the Jhelum as it still goes raging and fuming along at the bottom of the valley lamenting, say the Cashmeris, in foam and clamour its departure from their beautiful valley. At last we saw, on a raised plateau, a large mud fort which we knew was Uri whither we were bound. The dak bungalow was behind it, but first we had to descend into a valley to cross a little stream and then to scale the most fearfully stony road I ever saw. However, seeing the end in view, we addressed ourselves to the task before us and, having reached the top, came in at a canter which was a satisfactory ending to our march of eighteen miles over the roughest and steepest of roads.

The cook had already arrived and we had passed the coolies with the provender about half a mile from our goal. We are certainly improving in our arrangements every day; the cook and bhistie *(water-carrier)* now go on in front some hours before we start and the khansama comes on behind with the rest of the coolies, so that on this occasion, within half an hour of our arrival, we had a comforting breakfast of cocoa, rice, milk, hunter's beef and eggs with chupattis. The bungalow is prettily situated and is an improvement on the Chakoti one. It has just had new doors and window-shutters which, being made of pinewood, smell very sweet and clean. Glass is, of course, a luxury unknown in these parts. When we remember that the Maharajah charges nothing for the use of these rest-houses we are not disposed to criticize them too severely. It is a great boon to have even shelter provided, and though the tables and chairs are not much to boast of they are considerably better than nothing. The dak bungalows in British territory are not very much better as regards their furniture, and travellers have to pay a rupee a day for their accommodation, besides having to submit to the extortions of the harpies in charge.

From our veranda at Uri we had a splendid view of the snows, and the air was decidedly cool and pleasant as we had considerably increased our elevation during the last march. After tiffin we wandered off to explore our little plateau, from the edge of which we could see the Jhelum rushing along below as boisterous as ever, and here it was spanned by a most curious rope bridge. I gathered a nosegay of pomegranate flowers, white and yellow jasmine, the loveliest, tiniest pink roses, southernwood and many other flowers and scented herbs. Our pleasant occupation, however, was rudely interrupted by a sudden downfall of rain; it had been thundering and looking queer along the mountains for some minutes. We made for the house at full speed and reached it just in time to escape a good wetting - and then we began to think sadly of our bedding which was still on the road, but were soon cheered by seeing our packages arrive as the coolies straggled in one by one and quietly deposited their burdens in the veranda.

The storm was short and when it cleared up we went to inspect the Maharaja's fort, which is an astonishing looking building in an enclosed courtyard and though, owing to its commanding position, imposing from a distance, it presents by no means a martial appearance on closer acquaintance as it is built of mud and is very dilapidated. A sepoy *(soldier)* who was lounging about readily undertook to show us the place, and informed us that it was held by fifty men. As we only saw him and a boy, however, we found it difficult to believe this, but on enquiry he explained that they were all away at their work on the hillsides and, as they knew how to fight and were within call, they could easily be assembled in any emergency by a signal from the hilltop. I thought this a very sensible arrangement; what a huge burden would be removed from the nations of Europe if their immense forts could be occupied by a few men, while the rest of the vast garrisons could be within reach but earning an honest livelihood. There is this difference however; the Maharaja in his happy valley has no enemy watching for an opportunity to fly at this throat. In the fort was an ancient brass cannon with a Persian inscription on it, and some little iron ones that run on three wheels with the most curious powder flasks in the shape of fish belonging to them. This collection of weapons, though shown to us with great pride by the sepoy in charge, was certainly not very formidable, and would probably, if fired, do more damage inside the fort than out of it. There were also some enormous jars apparently of mud or clay, filled with grain. They were quite large enough to contain a man and I could now, for the first time in my life, quite imagine Ali Baba's forty thieves comfortably ensconced for the night in forty jars of this kind.

After a dinner of soup, partridge and rice pudding, we packed and arranged everything for an early start and went to bed. The storm must have made it cooler for we had not half enough coverings and we were shivering all night though doors and windows were closed and we were wrapped up in our dressing gowns.

In the morning we debated whether we should put on woollen or cotton garments and finally decided to risk wearing the latter for one day more, relying on exercise to keep us warm. We found it bitterly cold until we were warmed with a good walk, but after that we congratulated ourselves on having decided on light clothes.

There were some terrific ups and downs as usual but after a time the road lay along a pleasant fertile plain at a little elevation above the river which here widens out into a most magnificent torrent. Though wider, it seems more restless than ever, and goes foaming and churning along forming great whirlpools and surging round rocky islets. No boat could have lived a moment in it, though at one part we saw three men going down the rapids on mussacks *(inflated leather water bags)* taking advantage of every eddy and shelter to get across. Such power it seemed to me ought to be turned to account in some way, though I was not exactly prepared to say how it could be utilized - my husband suggested saw-mills for the pine forests.

The snows were in view at almost every turn and the wayside was clothed with loveliness as with a garment. The wild roses climbed over the trees, the ground was covered with jasmine blossoms, the chestnuts were in full bloom and the deodars were a joy for ever with their magnificent straight stems and their cold dark foliage, rising tier above tier to the very tops of the mountains.

On this march my husband walked the whole fourteen miles and I often joined him. About half way we saw a curiously carved stone by the roadside and, on looking round to find some reason for its being there, we discovered among the trees, all hidden with foliage, a handsome ruined gateway to which it had evidently belonged. After scrambling through this over rocks and briars we found the remains of a temple built of enormous blocks of a greenish grey limestone veined with white. It was foursquare and had a trefoil arch looking each way. There were steps up to the front but almost all traces of them were lost and overgrown, covered up by the thickest of undergrowth, and the place seemed entirely given up to desolation. The style was very massive and grand, the huge blocks being kept in position by their own weight without cement of any kind. The material was very beautiful, unlike anything I had ever seen before, and some of the blocks showed that it was capable of a high polish. From the temples which we afterwards saw, we are led to believe that it was a very ancient temple dedicated to the worship of the sun.

When we came to the road again we found that our syce and horse had gone on ahead and we had a good run to catch them. I can go downhill at a great rate but have no breath left after a climb, whereas my husband goes uphill or downhill like a mountain goat without the least apparent inconvenience.

On reaching Rampur we found the bungalow under repair and quite uninhabitable. There was only one whole chair in the place and of this our doctor friend had already taken possession, but he insisted on giving it up in my favour, a delicate attention which I was able to repay later on. Since leaving Hattian we had caught daily glimpses of our fellow traveller; he generally started rather earlier than we did, as he had not so much luggage to arrange and, besides, I hate early rising even in Cashmere. As there was not a single room in the bungalow which we could occupy, we sought for a spot on which to pitch our tents when they should come up. Opposite the rest-house was a charming little plateau at the foot of a mountain; above it rose forests of pines and chestnuts to the very summit. The place seemed to have been made by nature on purpose for camping; we put a stick in the ground to mark the spot where we wished our rent to be pitched and went to see what our cook was doing. We found that the khansama at the bungalow could make cakes, and when he brought us one for our inspection, as it really looked quite English of a kind, I promptly bought it and, breaking off great hunches, distributed them to my husband and our neighbour, who was like ourselves patiently waiting for his breakfast. We also got some milk to drink and so were able to satisfy our immediate cravings. Here in these hill countries we get a sharp eager appetite, but we never have the faint sinking feeling which we get in the plains of India when we have to wait for our food and then can hardly persuade ourselves to welcome it when it comes. Our breakfast was soon announced and we had it as well as we could in one of the wretched rooms with its mud floor, balancing ourselves on the rickety chairs that were literally not able to stand alone. We then returned to our terrace to await the arrival of our tents and luggage. It began to be cool and I wished they would come so that I could get into some warmer clothes. Meanwhile we followed the example of the coolies who had spread themselves abroad in various postures of repose; and with our railway rugs for a pillow we lay down in a shady place to rest and wait. My husband was soon sound asleep but, hearing thunder and noticing a gathering storm, I roused up the servants and, as soon as the tents arrived, ordered them to be pitched, as we and our luggage were really without proper shelter, the bungalow being all wet mud and mortar and entirely without doors and windows. I hurried on operations and things were drawing to a satisfactory conclusion when my husband suddenly awoke and, as quite a new discovery, announced a coming storm. Whilst he was speaking the rain was upon us and we had just time to rush into the half-erected tent, all our luggage being bundled in after us. There we sat in state on the bundles while the storm raged and our poor servants outside were patiently completing their work of driving in the pegs and tightening the ropes.

The storm was soon over and we were able to go outside and sit in the shade and look at the beautiful prospect which surrounded us on all sides. The place was so lovely and charming that I wanted to stay a day or two now that we had encamped, but my husband wished to get on to Srinagar and the servants, though marching on foot every day, did not seem to wish for a rest so we decided to start as usual in the morning. Our coolies were very willing souls; we had fifteen, of whom ten used to start when the moon rose and the other five left after us in the morning, bringing our tents, beds, and other belongings. We often watched them arranging their loads; it was amusing to see how they all made for the soft-looking bundles and avoided the heavy compact things.

When it got dark we had dinner in the bungalow because our tents were so far away from the bawarchikhana *(cookhouse)*, and then we went forth into the darkness up the mountainside to find our tent. The men being inexperienced in camping had not pitched it well and they had neglected to make a trench and mound round it, so that the frosty air came in from all directions. Tom was very cold and in consequence restless. I slept undisturbed except by my sympathy for him, but as he had every advantage which I had and far more bedclothes beside, I did not think it necessary to sympathise to any great extent.

At dawn we were stirring. I felt a great objection to getting up and dressing in the cold draughty tent. So I, who under the most favourable circumstances am averse to early rising, purposely lingered till seven o' clock when we started after a frugal breakfast. We dressed in woollen clothes and were glad to walk fast to get warm.

After a couple of hours' hard walking up the steep roads, however, my husband thought he should like to put on lighter clothes and, as he had taken the precaution on this march to bring a coolie boy with us who carried his dressing bag and a change of raiment, we stopped by the roadside in a retired nook while he made his toilet. We turned the horse out to graze, ate some chupattis which we had in our pockets, and Tom commenced operations in what he thought was a secluded spot, I sitting discreetly on the other side of a tree trunk receiving the discarded garments with averted gaze and packing them in the bag. Secluded as we thought ourselves, however, quite a small congregation assembled to watch the proceedings in which they took a most intelligent interest from beginning to end. Not a buckle or button escaped their scrutiny and finally, as the ceremony approached completion, a man came forward and proposed that he should shave the sahib. Tom readily agreed but, when he saw the razor which the man produced, a thing like a small two-edged axe, he withdrew from the bargain.

Razor

About two miles farther on we came to a place where we had milk which the villagers brought us in an earthenware vessel. It was delicious and we drank about a pint each. I gave the syce and coolie also as much milk as they cared for, and for all this we paid two annas, which the vendors of the milk thought extremely liberal. We now had about four miles to Baramulla and the whole way we were pestered with boatmen presenting their chitties *(written notes, testimonials)* and wanting us to engage them for the river journey to Srinagar. The road too became very trying; in fact it was the steepest bit we had had for the last fifty miles and we required all our breath for the difficulties of the way, and these men were consequently a great annoyance. My husband got quite angry but his wrath had not the slightest effect; we were joined at every turn by fresh groups and we finally entered Baramulla with a large mob at our heels.

We found our cook had extemporized a fireplace under a tree, and when we stopped near it we were encircled by a crowd of boatmen, women and children all gazing at us most unwinkingly and evidently finding us a great source of entertainment. We finally chose one boatman so as to get rid of the rest, and went on board his boat which was moored close by. It was large and roomy and had a roof of woven thatch, and curtains made of thick grass which we could let down at pleasure. While our luggage was being put on board we went ashore and had tiffin beneath the fixed and penetrating gaze of twelve men, three boys, one woman, two calves and two dogs.

The women here are of a very striking type of beauty. Many of them were grinding or winnowing corn and seemed pleased and friendly when we stopped to look at them. They have beautiful dark eyes and handsome massive features, their limbs too are large and robust and their movements stately and graceful. The children are pretty and attractive; they have often soft curly hair and the little girls have a most elaborate arrangement of long thin plaits which fall over their shoulders and are fastened together in a bunch just below the waist. At the point where their own hair fails they eke it out with black wool. The artifice is so transparent that it is easy to forgive it and there is really a certain grace about the arrangement, especially when it is crowned with the jaunty little red forage caps which they all wear.

It soon began to rain so we hastened to get our luggage and servants on board the boat and were quickly on our way up the river. We sent the horse by land, promising the syce a present if he brought him safe to us at Srinagar. The Jhelum river, whose course we have followed steadily all the week, has been slowly widening today and is now a broad placid river. It is really quite a relief to me to see it going along quietly and comfortably after having been so long a witness of its turbulence and unrest. Its voice has been ever in our ears even when we lost sight of it for a time and now, as we are being gently towed over its glassy surface, I can scarcely believe it is the same river. It seems strange that, contrary to the usual practice of rivers, it should become peaceful and navigable as it nears its source, but the secret of it is this. The legends of the country tell us that ages ago Cashmere was a lake. This is easy of belief for the whole valley, 100 miles long and from 25 to 35 miles wide, is entirely surrounded by mountains, at the foot of which in many places run long beach-like plateaus evidently formed by alluvial deposit and shelving downwards just like the shores of a lake. The legend says that Solomon visited the valley and, finding it filled with noxious water which had no outlet, he struck the mountain barrier at its weakest part, Baramulla, when the waters rushed out and tore for themselves the channel of the Jhelum, leaving to Cashmere its beautiful and fertile plains. However this may be, it is certain that through the single opening at Baramulla the Jhelum carries down to the Punjab the gathered streams and lakes of the entire basin. These, swollen by the snows of winter as well as by the copious rains of spring, rush through the narrow outlet down the steep and continuous descent, and this accounts for the tumultuous impetuosity manifested by this extraordinary river after leaving Cashmere.

As we passed along in our boat the immediate foreground struck us as very tame after the scenery through which we had come. Sometimes the ground was mildly undulating but generally the shores were flat, with fertile marshy-looking meadows and polled willows. We were still, however, surrounded by lofty mountains in the distance and we continually had splendid snow views in every direction.

CHAPTER 2

Our boat was a long roomy vehicle with an elaborately carved edge all round the part which we occupied; its thatched roof and its thick grass chicks *(grass blinds)* kept out both the cold and the sun. Our head boatman had blue eyes and fair hair which looked odd with his brown skin; his wife lived at the back of the boat where she did all the cooking in a small stove made of baked earth called a chula *(fireplace made of mud)*. There was a straw curtain between us, which was intended to give privacy to both establishments, but the intense curiosity of these people overcomes their sense of propriety and I often found a pair of large soft eyes fixed on me through a chink in the curtain.

Boat-towing

The man told us he had no children, which is a great desideratum in a boatman but there were three belonging either to him or to the man in the servants' boat which followed us. One, a girl about eleven years old, has a really beautiful face both in form and expression. She often helped to tow the boat and pulled away with a will, followed by her father and brother. They were harnessed with a rope round the chest, something like children playing horses. There were also two small boys named Sahmdoo and Mahindoo. The former, who was about five, was very fond of coming to talk to us and enquiring about our manners and customs; in return we enquired about his. When we asked him where his home was he pointed with one small brown forefinger at the deck of the boat and said 'Here'. He also told us that he ate rice and fish and that he sometimes had tea as a great treat. One evening, while he was with us, it began to grow chilly and his sister brought him a little basket fitted with an earthen pot containing burning charcoal. This he slipped under his garment with the ease of an habitué and squatted over it, evidently enjoying its warmth. These baskets are called kangris and are used by all Cashmeris of every age; they carry them wherever they go tucked away somewhere under their garments which, being of wool, keep in the heat especially when they are sitting down.

Mahindoo was a pretty boy of two with lovely dark eyes and curly hair. His only garment was a waistcoat that had evidently belonged to a tall stout Englishman, the curves of whose person 'cling to it still'. (His proud father informed us, upon enquiry, that it had been given him by a Colonel Thompson). Mahindoo's tiny proportions were utterly buried, in it; the waistcoat in fact trailed on the ground. His mother had not even troubled herself to make it fit him in any way so that he looked all armholes and pockets. When he landed in the evening for a romp with the other children he generally took it off so that it might not impede his sports; and then he put it on again, as likely as not with his head through one of the armholes.

The Cashmeris all dress in a loose ugly woollen garment of a dingy grey colour, which is most unbecoming to both figure and complexion. The Emperor Akbar is, I believe, responsible for this clumsy garment. When he conquered Cashmere in 1586 he dictated the dress of the people and they have worn it ever since. They wrap themselves up very much but they seem to think that their children require very little clothing and the smaller they are the less they give them.

When we want food the servants' boat, where they do all the cooking, is brought alongside and the khansama steps on board with a tray and arranges a meal. On the first day, just as tea had been brought us and we were exclaiming 'What luxury!', a sudden squall struck us and for five minutes everything was in the greatest confusion. The tea turned over, my diary flew into the water as also did Tom's coat that, with graceful abandon, he had taken off for the time being. The boat was at once pushed under shelter of the shore, but the storm fell as suddenly as it rose, our scattered possessions were picked up, and the diary and the coat were spread on the roof of the boat to dry. The tea was rearranged, and we subsided thankfully, but with the knowledge that we might expect certain variations in our life of dolce far niente.

The boat used to be anchored at sunset and we generally took a walk on shore. After dinner we let down the chicks and made ourselves snug and comfortable for the night. When we wake in the morning we find ourselves gliding along, as the men start at daybreak and there is no noise or movement to wake us. I sometimes opened a chick and watched the sun rise behind a mountain, but it was really nothing remarkable. I never can rave about sunrises; sunsets are as a rule incomparably finer and not nearly so much trouble to see.

The first night we stopped at a place called Sopor and in the morning found ourselves near the Wular Lake through which the Jhelum flows. This is the largest lake in Cashmere and it is subject to sudden and violent squalls of which the boatmen are justly afraid. The Maharaja Gulab Singh some 30 years ago was caught in one of these storms when crossing the lake and, though he himself escaped, many of his boats were wrecked and some hundreds of his retinue drowned. However, on this peaceful Sabbath day when we passed through it, its glassy surface was undisturbed save by the diving of water birds and the leaping of fish. It was adorned with myriads of white water lilies and with the pretty foliage of the singhara nut and other water plants. Our boat cut its way through all this loveliness for some hours. We now and then turned from the English letters which we were writing to gather lilies, some of the stalks of which were four yards long; the boatmen said they often grew to eight or nine yards.

Wular Lake

The singhara is a small horned nut which is very sweet and nourishing; it is dried and ground into flour and is a staple food of the people. On this lake alone thousands of tons are gathered every year and are an important source of revenue to the Maharaja who, with a charming simplicity in revenue arrangements, takes as his share half the produce thus avoiding all the trouble of fractions.

As we went floating placidly on we met a boatful of very noisy lively people going to a wedding. They fired guns - queer looking weapons with no end of barrel - at short intervals and of course took care to fire one just as they were passing us. The bridegroom reclined in the stern with an air of dignity and elegance combined; someone was holding a white cotton umbrella over him. There was no bride in the boat; the party was on its way to take possession of her.

We found if difficult to keep to the channel in this lake and occasionally ran aground but our boatmen soon pushed us off. They really manage their clumsy flat-bottomed craft with wonderful skill, as if to the manner born; whether paddling, or punting, or wading about in the shallows pushing us off a mud bank, or towing from the shore, they seem equally at home. The women who are strong and robust take their share in all the work, and the children are trained to help from their earliest years. They have little paddles given them in proportion to their size which they soon ply very cleverly, and they may often be seen harnessed to the towrope trotting along in front of their toiling parents with their hands full of poppies or irises, happy in the idea that they are helping to pull.

On the second evening we stopped at Shadipur, or 'the place of marriage', for here the river Sind runs into the Jhelum. Our boatmen anchored in what they thought a delightful spot among a lot of native boats, the smoke and smell of cooking from which were most offensive. We accordingly insisted on their going further up the river to a more open place, and when they said they were afraid of a storm we thought it all nonsense, for the river looked a broad, placid, harmless-enough looking stream. Just as we were preparing to go to rest, however, a squall burst upon us and nearly turned us over. Our things flew about in all directions, our camp table doubled up with a flap, the women and children - and the men too - groaned and cried and called upon 'Allah', and all we could do was to hold on bodily and be thankful that it was blowing towards the shore so that we were not likely to be driven from our moorings out into the cold dark river which had quite lost its harmless, placid appearance. In about ten minutes all the creaking and straining subsided and the men came to see how we were getting on with a triumphant 'I told you so' expression on their faces. We made a point of not seeming in the least frightened and chided them for making such an uproar about a puff of wind, but notwithstanding this hypocrisy I felt rather afraid to go to bed and was strongly inclined to sit up watching for another little tornado.

On the morning of the following day we found we were approaching Srinagar, the capital of Cashmere. We had scarcely looked in the glass all the week but now that we were nearing civilisation, our appearance caused us some concern, mine especially, as my nose had never recovered the roasting it got on the march from Hattian. I had just arisen from my couch and was sitting wrapped in my dressing gown, wondering what I could do to make myself presentable, when a voice from a neighbouring boat hailed us in unmistakable English and asked us if we should like some fish for our breakfast. We accepted readily and after some further conversation found that our benefactor was a Captain P. who was fishing in the river on his way up. He presently asked us if we knew anything of his luggage, which he had not seen for some weeks. Thanks to our habit of stopping every coolie on the road and enquiring to whom the baggage which formed his load belonged we were able to inform Captain P. that we had passed his belongings at Uri so that he might expect to see them in a day or two.

Bridge at Srinagar

As we approached Srinagar the river became very busy. The town is more quaint and picturesque-looking than anything I could have imagined. It is built on both sides of the river and communication is kept up by means of wooden bridges whose peculiar architecture greatly adds to the general effect. There are seven of them at irregular intervals and they are all built in the same way on great stacks of timber piled up with some attempt at regularity, but apparently not fastened in any way. Across these, pine trunks are laid and fastened with thongs of bark, and a light railing completes the structure. Some have as many as seven arches, others only three, and as may be imagined they are all of very irregular dimensions. The houses, five or six storeys high, are built of wood and are in all stages of dilapidation; they lean towards each other at every conceivable angle, and their outlines are everywhere broken by queer artistic-looking galleries and balconies.

Srinagar riverside

Scarcely a straight line is to be seen and it is a mystery how the various structures manage to hang together. You may see a frail-looking erection, supported apparently only on two crooked sticks and looking as if it were on the point of falling, which is yet full to overflowing of fat turbaned men who sit in the rickety looking balconies securely gazing down upon you as you pass. Many of these men were merchants on the lookout for visitors coming up the river and, thinking we looked like probable customers, they dispatched some of their myrmidons in boats to board us and show us their wares.

We were soon surrounded by little boats whose occupants were holding up all sorts of beautiful things with a view to tempt us; some of them even seized our boat and tried to come on board. For some time we were firm in declining these troublesome attentions, but at length we succumbed entirely to the blandishments of a portly old individual called

Sunnund Shah, a merchant banker of a most benevolent, avuncular appearance. His manners were smiling and bland, and though our reason told us that his kind solicitude could not be entirely disinterested, yet our feelings were so soothed by his sympathetic interest that, when he left us, we found to our astonishment that we had given all our money into his keeping and had taken his advice implicitly on all sorts of matters.

He informed us that the Munshi Bagh, *(Ed. – where the family of Oliver John Sykes, the diarist's second son, lived 1912-1916)* the usual camping ground for Europeans, was so full that we had better go on to the Ram Munshi Bagh. This proved to be a good deal further up the river and by the time we got there it was raining fast. Waterproofs had to be hastily fished out before we could sally forth to choose a camping ground. Having done this, we returned to the boat for shelter while the tents were being pitched, and employed the interval in devouring some bread and butter which our khansama had procured for us on our way up the river and, as it was several days since we had seen such luxuries, there was very little left of a loaf when we at last arose refreshed and strengthened.

Although it was raining steadily our tents were soon surrounded by men with all sorts of wares for sale. We had sternly ordered off all the boats that followed us, refusing even to look at a single article. The men landed, however, and hovered about us unobserved, and during the bustle of settling, when my husband happened to require a pen and ink to sign a notice that was brought him, one of these unobtrusive-looking individuals stepped forward with the required article. After making use of his pen we entered into conversation with him and presently he quietly produced a beautiful silver tray for our inspection, and we found he was one of the men whom we had so summarily and angrily dismissed on the river. His myrmidons appeared as if by magic and spread all sorts of tempting things on the ground around us. Other merchants also drew near and we amused ourselves with looking at their different wares and finally got rid of them by promising to visit their various shops on the morrow.

Munshi Bagh

On the following morning our benevolent, avuncular friend Sunnund Shah appeared early to conduct us to the shops. Having not yet made arrangements for a small boat we took to our large one again and went down the river at great speed, paddled by ten men, feeling very imposing and reminding ourselves of Anthony and Cleopatra going in state down the Nile. We were followed by a perfect fleet of boats full of people showing us specimens of their goods, and pressing us to visit their shops. When we landed we were surrounded by a large and lively mob persecuting us to buy, which was most annoying and irritating and interfered sensibly with the pleasure of shopping and sightseeing.

The best shops were those of the shawl merchants, of which Sunnund Shah's was a good specimen. After landing at a flight of steps we passed upward through various courtyards and landings, ornamented with shrubs and flowers in pots, till we found ourselves in a cool airy apartment overlooking the river, arranged with chairs and divans for the reception of customers. The walls were lined with miles of shawls, carpets and curtains in every variety of colour. We were received with much courtesy by another brother belonging to the firm named Rizul Shah; both brothers are fair, ruddy and handsome blue-eyed men and, with their smooth manners and spotless clothing, reminded us irresistibly of the merchants in the Arabian Nights. After offering us tea and sweetmeats they began to unfold and display the treasures that surrounded us, gently pointing out their beauties and dilating caressingly on their merits and value. The texture and designs of many of the things were very beautiful and artistic. Sometimes the tints were violent and garish but generally, in all the better and more expensive things, the colours though brilliant were perfectly harmonious.

From here we went to a papier-mâché merchant's where we bought a number of little trays and jars and some of the curious Cashmere pen boxes. There are elegant little tables and wall brackets in this work, and all sorts of knick-knacks, and the designs were very delicate and pretty. We afterwards went to buy some enamelled ware – dark and light blue and gold on copper, which is very handsome and effective. We disagreed with the man about the price, however, and left without buying anything, but sometime after, as we were returning home feeling rather sad that we had not our enamelled ware, a boat suddenly pulled up alongside us and lo, there was our plausible friend the merchant with the very things we coveted. To save ourselves from future regrets we concluded the bargain then and there.

It was nearly evening when we returned to our encampment and, as it began to rain soon after, we were obliged to have dinner in our tent. As we sat dolefully listening to the rain pattering down on to its frail roof my husband, wishing to be cheerful, said 'How glad they would be to have this rain in Lucknow' to which well-intentioned remark I replied 'How I wish they had it!' The rain however did not trouble us much. It is not nearly such a serious matter when encamping as it is in India; the showers are gentle and intermittent and there is a good deal of sunshine between, which soon dries the ground.

The place where we had encamped was a large orchard on the banks of the river and here we spent a most delightful browsing kind of existence reading, writing, talking, sketching, lounging on the grass and feeling as if we had neither cares nor duties - as if, in fact, we had reached 'a land in which it seemed always afternoon'. Grape vines with enormous stems wandered from one tree to another making bowers of shade. These bore only promise of fruit, but the mulberries were ripe and in great profusion, and the apples were getting so large that my imagination saw a tart in the near future. The mulberries were very delicious, not so rich and luscious as English ones but more like a very fine kind of blackberry. We ate a great many of them following the example of all the inhabitants of Cashmere both man and beast, for not only were men, women and children always holding high carnival under the mulberries trees but the cattle devoured them with great relish, and they were used as bait even for the fish.

We lived almost entirely in the open air, and when once we had managed to choke off the itinerant vendors who tormented us, by beating down their prices to a point that was positively insulting, we found the sweet, solitary, rural life most congenial. The broad river flowed past us within a few yards distance, but it was hidden from our view by its high banks, and so gentle was its current that we could not even hear the murmur of its voice. The sun was often hot in the middle of the day, but we could always get shade and there was generally a cool breeze tempered by the snow-capped mountains which surround the valley of Cashmere on every side, and which were nearly always visible, especially at sunrise and sunset.

In our immediate neighbourhood was an imposing looking hill called Takht-i-

Suleiman, the throne of Solomon, crowned by a Bhuddhist temple of great antiquity that is now used as a Hindu temple. The Takht is upwards of 1000 feet high. It looked very near to us and, as day after day we saw it in all its various moods, smiling in the sunshine and frowning in the storm, we felt that sooner or later we should have to climb it. We often took long pleasant walks in the evenings and could almost fancy ourselves in England; the fields were full of poppies and not only English flowers but English weeds abounded on every hand. My delight in these apparently amused my husband, for he presently presented me with a small bouquet composed of dandelions and nettles. This display of what he thought humour, however, did not quench my enthusiasm at recognizing these old friends of my childhood.

The river winds about in the most extraordinary manner and we were constantly meeting it in most unexpected directions. In fact the particular curve in which we were encamped is said to have given rise to what is called 'the pine pattern', which for hundreds of years has figured so largely in the beautiful Cashmere shawls and which is used too in most of the other manufactures of the place. During our wanderings one evening we came suddenly upon a gentleman and a lady who, being on their way up-river to Islamabad, had just landed from their boat for a stroll. He was up a tree birds-nesting and she had her hands full of poppies and purple irises. We were all of us rather carelessly attired and had no need to apologise to each other, but our friend carried off the palm for unconventionality, for he had neither hat nor coat on, having left them in the boat, and apparently had not shaved for a week. We found they were the same people whom we had met at Sopor and who had given us some fish. It was very pleasant to meet again and compare impressions and after a little lively chat we went our several ways.

The charm of this simple primitive kind of life grew upon us daily; we began to scorn the trammels of civilisation and to be almost eager for a return to skins and woad. We had never lived much in tents and felt, notwithstanding our mature age, as if we were children playing at camping out. Many of the words and ways of our childhood came back to us quite naturally. The sight of some willows near us suddenly inspired Tom with a desire to make some whistles such as he used to be a dab at when a boy, and he spent one whole morning in making whistles from willow wands. Each was more successful than the last, a success which I bitterly regretted as I was expected to sit and listen urbanely to the ear-piercing shrieks which he ever and anon produced with such unfeigned pride and pleasure that I had not the heart to dampen his ardour. I did venture to remark that I was afraid he would rouse the neighbourhood but, as the neighbourhood consisted only of herds of cows and flocks of sheep and goats with boys and girls engaged in thwacking them at intervals, he did not think it worthy of much consideration, so he continued to make the day hideous with his whistles and for the time being our quiet retreat seemed to have become a busy railway junction.

We were not quite cut off from the world, however, as we sometimes got English letters from our far-off children and friends, and some nice people who were camping near us, and with whom we kept up a gentle intermittent kind of intercourse, constantly sent us batches of English and Indian papers. We had discharged our boatman soon after we had arrived as they and their families began to be very troublesome. I had first talked to the children and had given them little presents of money and they often brought me mulberries and flowers. This pleased me until I saw plainly that it was prompted by their parents, and all the grace of the action vanished when I perceived hard by the greedy eyes of those parents watching for the expected result, namely baksheesh. A great deal of the pleasure of travelling in this country is spoilt by the constant demand of baksheesh. The people don't take the least trouble to disguise the fact that they regard travellers only as a prey; they are perfectly insatiable and whatever you give them they seem to expect more. If you took the least kindly notice of or interest in them, they become troublesome and intrusive. We know that, in a measure, gratitude is a sense of favours to come all the world over.

Still, the barefaced and continuous exhibition of this fact turned the milk of human kindness in my nature to gall, and I positively began to detest those boatmen and their belongings. We were never free from them. They followed us into every shop to see what we bought and to demand dustoori *(commission or customary fee)*; if merchants came to our tents they stood round watching the proceedings with evident intention. Accordingly, we went once down the river to arrange some little business and on our return paid them liberally, gave them chitties and told them to go. They were very clamorous and grasping but at last they went and we breathed freely and gave ourselves up to peace and rest.

The climate was very much like a fine summer's day in England. It sometimes grew hot, but a cool refreshing breeze was sure to spring up before long. The air was bracing too and we used to come home after our evening walk gloriously tired and hungry to enjoy our dinner under the trees in the twilight. Then we would have our lamp lighted and Tom would smoke and I would read aloud till we were tired enough for bed. After about a week of this lotus-eating life we were stirred up by a notice from the Chaplain that service would be held in the little church at the Sheik Bagh on the following day. He also sent round a clock from which the time of the service was to be taken and at which we were invited to look. This struck me as being a very canny arrangement on his part for, as everyone in Srinagar was a law unto himself with regard to the time, there would have been great confusion if they had all gone to church at the time as recorded by their own watches.

On Sunday morning, accordingly, we engaged a boat and made a great effort to return to something like civilisation by going to church. The sola topis *(pith helmets)* and various shabby garments in which we had been luxuriating were laid aside and we issued forth from our tent in slightly creased but immaculate suits of Sunday-best. We glided gently down the river to the Sheik Bagh and, being early, we strolled over to the little cemetery. Most of the graves were those of young officers who had died while visiting Cashmere and the monuments had been erected by their brothers-in-arms. The church is the upper storey of the chaplain's house and has a curious inlaid domed roof. It has windows all round of carved lattice-work through which the sweet air comes pleasantly; as there is no glass, however, the service in winter has to be held in some more sheltered place but, as at that time there are few residents and scarcely any visitors in Srinagar, that is easily arranged.

The service was most simple and primitive, which was as it should be considering the simple and primitive surroundings, but it was read in a hesitating muddled way without the least impressiveness. The sermon too was poor and badly delivered. Why is it that clergymen are often such poor creatures at the work for which they are set apart and to preparation for which they have devoted some years of their life? Any intelligent schoolboy could read better than many of them, any man of ordinary ability could produce a weekly discourse far above the average of those presented to us by our spiritual instructors. They have such a vast and momentous theme - religion, its bearing on life and death - they have no lack of hearers willing and anxious to be taught. There is the continual movement and suggestiveness of life around them, the world of books at their command, and it is only the most stupendous dullness that can produce the platitudes, the feeble twaddle, the weak recapitulation of the weighty truths of religion week after week which church-going people have put before them in a way which takes from them all nobleness, all beauty and almost all truth. I sit and listen and say:

'Oh brother man that patterest ancient sayings
At me thy brother man who mutely hears,
Is this the poor result of all thy prayings?
Hast thou no better harvest of the years?'

When I have gone to church burdened and perplexed with the cares and unsatisfactoriness of life, hoping and longing for some word that should strengthen and enlighten me, as wise and noble words can do, and have heard a sermon on Apostolic succession, or on Simon the Canaanite, or the Nicolaitans, I have turned away unsatisfied saying bitterly, 'I asked for bread and ye gave me a stone'. 'Tis true, as old George Herbert says, that in church,

'If all want sense
God takes a text and preacheth patience.
And he that gets patience and the blessing which
Preachers conclude with hath not lost his pains'.

Still, this is poor consolation when we might have so much more, and I am driven back on my conclusion that clergymen have such a splendid chance and that it is a marvel to me how the great majority of them manage to miss it completely.

We felt encouraged to repeat our efforts at returning to the amenities of life and spent the next morning in calling on the Resident. It is perhaps necessary here to state who the Resident is and how he came to exist, and to do this clearly we must go back about forty years. At the end of the first Sikh War, Gulab Singh, who had been Viceroy of Jammu under Ranjeet Singh, the great Sikh chieftain, and who had conquered Ladakh on his own account, offered the British Government one million sterling provided he were recognized as the Maharaja of those territories and of the Valley of Cashmere. It suited the English just then to accept those proposals and the bargain was concluded. From that time the Maharaja has been the ally and protégé of the British Government on condition of recognizing its supremacy and paying a nominal tribute. It was afterwards arranged that a British officer should reside at Srinagar to assist the Maharaja with advice and to remind him of the paramount power which, though it fully recognises his undisputed sovereignty and is careful not to fetter him in any way, would not scruple to interfere in case of any palpable misgovernment and oppression. In fact, the Maharaja is obliged to regulate his foreign policy according to the views of the Government of India, while in domestic administration he is nearly independent. This officer is called the Resident and there is also an English doctor and chaplain. The Residency is a long, low, two-storeyed building on the banks of the river, with picturesque gables and verandas, and balconies all built of pine wood; it is artistic both in design and colouring. We called at the residences of these officials, found the ladies at home in each instance and had an agreeable morning. We were afterwards invited to a dance at the Residency but as by that time we had commenced our wanderings in the Sind Valley, we had to refuse.

On the Queen's Birthday, however, which happened while we were in Srinagar, the Maharaja gave a grand dinner and nautch *(performance of a traditional dance by professional dancing girls)* to the English residents and visitors, to which we were invited. The entertainment was given at the Maundy Palace, which is situated by the riverside nearly opposite the Residency, and was built by the Maharaja for Lord Ripon when he paid him a visit. We went down in our little boat noiselessly through the darkness, and just before we got there we met the Resident's boat returning, which told us that we were late. The Resident has always two or three boats provided by the Rajah moored near his house. They are very gorgeous and are like floating pavilions covered with lacquer-work and fitted up with brilliant upholstery; when rowed by about thirty men all dressed in red they have a very imposing appearance.

The whole façade of the palace was illuminated and was perfectly reflected in the river. The palace itself is rather a gimcrack edifice with a plenitude of red and green pillars. As we landed at the broad flight of steps we were received by a gorgeous official; our way was marked out by red cloth and lined by troops. Being rather late we slipped into our places as people were sitting down to dinner. The Maharaja had received his guests and came for a little time into the dining room but disappeared with his suite when the repast began. The dinner was good and well cooked and served à la Russe; the courses seemed innumerable and the service was rather slow. The table decorations were very striking and effective, a broad strip of cloth of gold down the centre with large bowls of red poppies and lamps with crimson shades at intervals, while scattered about artistically were the graceful chenar leaves with their pretty green fluffy balls. This, though rather brilliant, harmonized well with the walls of the room which were covered with arabesque patterns in green and red which, though probably rather tawdry by daylight, looked well when lighted up.

More than a hundred guests were present, principally visitors to Cashmere, but besides these and the officials above-mentioned, there were various English officers both civil and military who are employed by the Maharaja in different capacities, principally road-making and engineering. At the dessert stage, the Maharaja reappeared and the health of the Queen Empress was proposed by the Resident. This being drunk, he proposed the health of the Maharaja, the giver of the feast, and after this had been drunk he returned thanks in the name of the Maharaja. This was, I thought, a great mistake on the part of the Resident. It was treating the Maharaja too much like a puppet. He should have been urged to return thanks on his own account even if it had been by the mouth of one of his suite, and in his own language which could easily have been translated.

After this we dispersed into the veranda which overlooked the river and the decorations of which were in the same style as those of the dining room. The visitors clustered in groups down the sides of the long room, the Maharaja with the Resident surrounded by their respective suites occupying a dais, provided with specially gorgeous chairs, at one end, the other end of the room being occupied by native musicians sitting on the floor who were to accompany the nautch.

Presently two Cashmeri girls rather overloaded with clothes and jewels appeared. They ambled slowly up and down the room to the sound of the music, their heavy silver anklets clanking melodiously as they moved. The principal display of grace was in the slow and elegant movements of their exceedingly beautiful hands and wrists; their fingers were loaded with rings and deeply dyed with henna. Other girls sat among the musicians waiting to take their turn in the dance, some of whom were really beautiful. They have all a Jewish cast of countenance - straight dark brows, good noses, large liquid eyes. In fact, it is a grand harmonious style of beauty, and I cannot help thinking that they are descended from some of the lost ten tribes. The performance was monotonous; they seemed as if they were going on for ever, as Aliph Cheem says:

'Advancing, retiring, uplifting their arms,
Now mimicking joy and feigning alarms,
Now figuring love, and portraying disdain,
and doing it over and over again.'

The music – which came from the most extraordinary-looking instruments, probably sackbuts, psalteries and dulcimers - alternately wailed and rejoiced for some time. Then the women burst forth into what they call song. It was very unrestrained and not melodious according to our notions but, as the voices rose and fell, now soft and pleading now passionate and complaining, I could imagine it having an influence on anyone who deliberately chose to think it beautiful. However, how it is that

'the nautch's voluptuous mazes can turn a man's brain
and allure him to blazes',

I am at a loss to imagine!

Presently fireworks began to go off from boats moored in the river. They were disappointing however - there was a great deal of noise and smoke but little else. When the Maharaja rose to leave, the Resident conducted him down the room and the company soon after separated. The scene at the landing stage was very lively, the boatmen all shouting and urging their boats to the front, but very soon everybody had embarked and disappeared into the darkness and silence.

Soon after this, feeling inclined for a little change in our mode of life, we decided upon an expedition to the Dal Lake. We ordered our boat to be in readiness, so the servants conveyed thither our beds, tables and chairs and what luggage was necessary for a couple of days, and we stepped on board. As we were doing so I noticed a large lump of yellowish clay which had been scooped up out of the river's bank and which they were carrying to the back or kitchen part of the boat. On enquiry what it was for, I found it was going to be modelled into a chula, whereon our food was to be cooked. Life seems so extremely simple in these parts; we began to think with scorn of our elaborate civilization which renders life so difficult and complicated.

Meanwhile we had started on our placid way. The morning was gloriously fresh and fine; for the day or two past there had been rain which had cooled the air, and the clouds that had been hanging about had disappeared, or only a pleasant white fleecy suggestion of them remained. We had just received a batch of English and Indian papers after a month's deprivation of news, so that our circumstances were specially happy and as we gently floated down the river watching the gay and picturesque crowds on its banks, the words of the poet composed in reference to this very spot rose to my lips:

'And oh if there be an Elysium on earth,
It is this, it is this'

Just opposite the palace we turned into a canal, on the banks of which are several handsome temples and other buildings. The interest and amusements of our way never flagged; we met such quaint boatloads of men who might have been Joseph's brethren, and once one handsome bearded man reclining alone in his glory who looked like Joseph himself. The men here all have a very Israelitish cast of countenance - our own boatmen we have named Gad and Asher. We passed flocks of fresh healthy-looking ducks and of robust energetic-looking geese, and we came upon bevies of sweet little girl children - mere babies - bathing and playing in the quiet pools while their mothers gossiped and kept an eye on them from the bank.

We came soon to the Chenar Bagh, which is a perfectly idyllic bachelor's encampment sheltered by poplars and chenars, and presently we found ourselves at the wooden gates in the long high causeway which separates the Dal Lake from the river. This structure was thrown up by the Muhammadans, and repaired and heightened by the late Maharaja. Its object is to keep the waters of the Jhelum under restraint during the floods. So long as the river is low, the gates are open but, as the water rises, the current of the stream closes the doors and the water is prevented from flowing into the lake - otherwise the overflow would probably flood the city. The gates looked very massive and primitive, and we had a great struggle to get through as the water from the lake came rushing out as soon as they were opened. However, we all lent a hand to the pushing and pulling and soon we were going on our quiet way again, at first between what looked like fields of osiers, but soon these disappeared and there was nothing to obstruct our view.

We appeared to be passing over forests of the loveliest waterweeds, which waved and shimmered beneath us. The water was as clear as air and the sun shone straight down into the depths, disclosing such combinations of greens and browns, and such families of active little fishes, as filled my eye and soul with delight. But our ecstasies made us hungry and we called for tiffin. It consisted of cold pigeon pie and other dainties and we amused ourselves as we ate by throwing the bones to the fishes and watching them struggle for them. But, alas, my husband soon began to feel very ill and had an attack of what he called seasickness, which effectually quenched his enjoyment. However, there was not a ripple on the lake, and as he is an exceptionally good sailor and, besides, he had been ill in the same way once before during our stay in Srinagar, I began to cast about in my mind for the cause of these attacks. At last I remembered that on such occasions we had had fish for breakfast, of which he had eaten heartily. On enquiry, I found that fish caught in the river below Srinagar is not considered good for food, and often makes Europeans ill. We resolved to have no more fish, but meanwhile, as my companion for some hours lay prone upon his bed absorbed in his own sufferings, I had to bottle my delight somewhat. I amused myself in gathering up specimens of the different waterweeds. Even out of the water they were lovely and in their native element they were indeed things of beauty. Myriads of dragonflies flitted about, of a vivid steely blue or a warm golden-brown.

Boats full of little brown children floated about among the water lilies. The patriarchs of the party, aged from six to ten years, would be paddling and managing the boat, and the younger ones would be taking care of the babies who were remarkably sleek and prosperous looking. The boat population of Srinagar seems to be almost amphibious; they are at home on the water from their birth and many of them know no other home. The children have tiny paddles given them before they can walk with which they are supposed to help to propel the boat. It is very pretty to see them emulating their parents, who look on with pride at their proficiency.

The Dal Lake is about five miles long by two and a half broad and is surrounded by mountains which are reflected in its waters with wonderful clearness. When we first entered its waters we found ourselves on the other side of the Takht-i-Suleiman, which had for some weeks been a familiar feature in our landscape, but from another point of view. At the foot of this mountain is a spring of clear water where the most costly Cashmere shawls are brought to be washed. We landed and found six hanging out to dry. The patterns were intricate and beautiful and they were of costly hand manufacture, but I did not covet any of them.

Going a little further we called at a house on the borders of the lake occupied by Suraj Bal who, a few months ago, was Chief Justice of Cashmere, but who is now superseded and somewhat out of favour. He was educated at Oxford University. His house is very handsome and is charmingly situated. His grounds, too, were prettier and better tended than any I have seen in Cashmere. Tom had an introduction to him but he was out, so we did not see him.

Dal Lake

Farther on still we came to a summer palace of the Maharaja's called the Nishat Bagh. It is a square building with verandas and colonnades of carved and coloured wooden pillars, and has square towers at each corner. The garden behind it rises in terraces up the sides of the mountain. There are arrangements for fountains and a succession of waterfalls, which must be very pretty when the water is turned on and the place illuminated. A great deal of this beauty is, however, left to the imagination of casual daylight visitors, and what really interested me most were the cherry trees, real English cherries, but alas still green. On one tree, however, they were turning red and I insisted on having a branch broken off which I greedily conveyed to the boat where I sat and ate the cherries with involuntary contortions of countenance, trying to think they were nice. Living in India as we do we, of course, never see many of the commonest English fruits and flowers, and this explains our childish delight in anything English. The Nishat Bagh was very hot indeed as the mountainside faced the afternoon sun, so we resolved to go on to the far famed Shalimar Gardens, whose beauties have been sung so melodiously by Moore in his 'light of the Harem'. On our way we had to pass under a most unique bridge. When the Muhammadans possessed the country they made a causeway across the lake which still exists, though submerged here and there and overgrown with trees and bushes. There are raised bridges in it at intervals, of a single arch, for boats to pass through, which look sometimes as if they came from nowhere and went nowhither like Addison's 'Bridge of Mirza'.

As we approached the 'Magnificent Shalimar' we found ourselves in a canal which soon became so choked with sedge and morass that we were obliged to leave our boats and walk the rest of the distance. The sun was setting and the thick creeping mists that hung about, as well as the smell from the decaying vegetation, warned us that it would not be safe to sleep on the water in our boat as we had intended to do. So, finding that Nourmahal's garden was well-raised above the miasma and that the handsome black marble pavilion at the far end of it was in good repair, we determined to have our beds carried thither from the boat which had stopped about a quarter of a mile away, and spend the night in this romantic spot which, as every school girl knows, is the place where the Emperor Jehangir made up his quarrel with 'his Nourmahal his harem's light'.

The gardens are very fine, laid out according to the Muhammadan custom in terraces rising one above another with large square pavilions on each terrace, which are surrounded by most elaborate arrangements for fountains and waterfalls. The grand and final pavilion is isolated in the midst of a marble basin, and is only to be approached by raised marble causeways terminating in one small flight of steps in front. It is built of large blocks of black marble, supported by massive and handsomely carved pillars. It is surrounded by fruit trees - cherries, apples, pears, and plums - and by flowering shrubs. There are many splendid chenars too, with their dense masses of foliage. These trees are so magnificent, such features in the landscape that it is impossible to avoid mentioning them in describing any place where they occur. The chenar is a kind of plane tree. It has large deeply indented leaves, its fruit is in the shape of little green fluffy balls, which, later on, turn to a golden brown and are very pretty in every stage. It grows to a great height and size, dwarfing all other trees and reminding me among them of a cathedral among ordinary houses. Its foliage is very dense and quite impervious to the rays of the sun. The trunks of many that we measured exceeded sixty feet in circumference. The bark is smooth and light-coloured and I don't think the wood is good for much as the branches snap in a storm, and the trunks are almost invariably hollow when the tree has grown to any size.

As darkness was coming on we took a hurried repast on the marshy banks of the canal and then went forward to wait while the servants transported our belongings to the pavilion, which was the work of an hour or so. They, of course, required our only lantern and we meanwhile sat on the marble steps feasting on our very romantic surroundings, lighted by a timid moon and thinking of Nourmahal and Jehangir from when:

'Alas, how light a cause had moved

Dissension between hearts that loved'

to when:

'Happier now for all her sighs
As on his arm her head reposes,
She whispers him with laughing eyes,
Remember love the Feast of Roses'.

The garden was equally beautiful in the early dawn and after wandering through it and startling the herons, which were roosting after their uncomfortable fashion in some of the trees, we went on board our boat and were soon making our way to the Nasim Bagh. The water in this part of the lake is very deep, some thirty or forty feet, and is quite free from the weeds and water lilies that abound in other parts. The Nasim Bagh is merely a grove of several hundred chenars, all enormous specimens of their kind and nearly all hollow. There are traces of a flight of steps for landing and the bank of the lake slopes gently upward.

Quite a large colony of English visitors was encamped among the trees. There were tents of all sorts and sizes, some with very elaborate appointments such as lace curtains and hanging baskets of ferns, others disclosing merely the familiar camp bed and chillumchee *(washbasin of brass or tinned copper)*, telling of the stern simplicity of bachelor life. We strolled round this delightful spot, saw the Tennis and Polo Ground and were amused to note that some of the hollow trees had been utilised as dressing and bath rooms; a chick or straw curtain, hung before the opening, rendered them quite private.

On our return to the boat we found that our khansama and cook being Muhammadans had seized the opportunity of our absence to visit a ziarat, as the mosques in these parts are called, where there is preserved, in a glass phial with a silver top, a hair from the beard of the prophet Mahomet. This ziarat is called Hazrat Bal and is considered very sacred. The relic, however, is only exhibited at great festivals so our servants returned disappointed not having seen it. As we passed the place, soon after having started again on our homeward voyage, they pointed it out to us with great reverence. It was a large and handsome building but, like all buildings in these parts, very much dilapidated. The peculiarity of this and other Eastern nations is that, though they design and execute magnificent buildings at enormous cost, they don't recognise the necessity of keeping them in repair, and from the day they are finished they are left to the action of time without the slightest effort being made to arrest the progress of decay. This is partly from want of energy and partly from selfishness. No one cares to take trouble to perpetuate any name but his own. I have seen in India a massive tower begun, with the idea of handing his name to posterity, by a king who died when it had reached a certain height, and his son and successor, instead of thinking it a pious duty to carry out his father's unfinished work, immediately set about building a similar tower on his own account. His son and successor followed his example, so that there are three of these monuments side by side in various stages of incompleteness, all testifying to the short-sighted selfishness of their founders. We English are trying to teach the various peoples who come under our rule that the best way to raise monuments that will perpetuate their memory is to found institutions for the good of their fellow men, that will go on living after they are dead - and the hospitals and colleges having native founders that adorn many of the principal towns in India show that they are learning this lesson.

The floating gardens of the lake, about which a good deal has been written, are not very romantic in appearance and rather injure than enhance the scenery. They are simply beds of rushes with earth sprinkled over them, rendered compact by large clumps of a mossy weed being spread over them and moored by means of long poles to a clear spot in the lake! They are very fertile and cucumbers, tomatoes and most English vegetables are grown on them.

Having completed the circuit of the lake we soon found ourselves outside the wooden gates and on our way up the river. It was morning and the whole population of Srinagar seemed to be performing its toilet on the river banks. Now it was a woman washing herself and her clothes, or giving her unfortunate baby a most uncompromising scrubbing, or a man cleaning his teeth with a stick and some charcoal. Our boat passed in and out among the bathers without causing them any surprise or inconvenience, sometimes through a group of merry brown urchins splashing or diving like fishes, and sometimes among laughing girls who tried to hide themselves behind each other or in the shelter of a neighbouring boat from which, however, they would peep out to watch our progress. Occasionally a fat bald man would pop up beside our boat and calmly proceed with his ablutions eyeing us the while, and quite regardless of the fact that we also were eyeing him. At a little distance we saw a pretty baby boy sitting in a boat with his mother and, in reaching for some trifle floating past him, he fell into the river, which was here both deep and broad. The mother did not seem in the least alarmed and, clutching him by one of his little limbs, soon had him safe on board again. The child spluttered and whimpered for a minute or two but when we passed he had quite recovered and was only tearfully regarding his little shirt that had been taken off and was hanging out to dry. I never saw people dress so quickly. They come out of the water dripping and glittering, pick up their dingy drab garment, slip into it like a flash, pop on their dirty cap or turban, and look out at you dressed. It seemed strange that we were not shocked al all by this display of puris naturalibus, but we were able to regard it with unfeigned interest and amusement. This must have been because of the brown skins of the people, which seem in a sense to be a covering unto them, for when an unusually fair pale-skinned man appeared we felt a thrill through all our being which showed that our native modesty was not yet dead.

We reached our encampment at noon and felt as if we had got home for the time being. The next day we called on some Lucknow friends who are visitors like ourselves but are living in a bungalow and have made themselves very comfortable. It is nice to be surrounded by pretty things - their room looked quite luxurious after our strictly necessary surroundings. Still, every time we move I am glad to have so few impedimenta.

In the evening we walked to see an old temple quite near our encampment, which was built some 200 years B.C. and is composed of large hewn stones held together by their own weight without cement or plaster of any kind. It stands in the middle of a small lake and is a perfect picture of desolation. A tree grows out from its roof and is evidently displacing the stones. While I took a rough sketch of it, Tom crossed the water in a crazy little boat and went inside. The interior consists of one room and, as the twilight was falling rapidly, he saw little but darkness. The water was green and slimy and the temple itself was literally a habitation for owls and bats, which flapped about uneasily while we remained. Though this shrine has for centuries been deserted and its altar cold, yet it doubtless fulfilled its mission in ages gone by to some seekers after God, in those times of ignorance which we are told God winked at. This temple of Pandrilan, like many others whose ruins one sees in Cashmere, seem to have been dedicated to the Nag, or snake worship. It was placed in the centre of a tank so that it might be under the protection of the snake who was supposed to inhabit the spring. The worship of natural objects such as snakes, trees, springs or the sun is probably the earliest known form of worship. Of all these I can best understand the worship of the sun, 'that beam of the eternal beam'. To people who had had no revelation, it would seem the most natural thing possible to greet his glorious uprising with worship, seeing that it was from his beams they received most of the blessings which made their primitive lives worth living.

We had now been in Srinagar more than a fortnight and were beginning to think of fresh fields and pastures new. We decided, however, to wait till the English mail had come in before we made a move, and meanwhile the Takht, crowned with its temple, still looked down upon us, unconquered and unexplored. Had I been left to myself I should have been quite content with seeing it from below, and with imagining all that was to be seen from the top, but my husband's painfully energetic nature thought foul scorn of such ignoble compromise and, in a weak moment, I promised to go up with him whenever he liked. Accordingly, the very next morning I was roused at 4 a.m. Induced by a mixture of bullying and coaxing to dress and drink some tea, I presently found myself floating down the river in a most meek and dejected frame of mind, wishing the Takht had never been heard of. We landed at the foot of the hill and the ascent immediately commenced. The whole way is composed of very rough and irregular stone steps up which I plodded steadily and painfully for an hour and, by turning occasionally to look at the view and by not wasting my breath in conversation, I managed to get to the top - but it was a frightful effort. Tom, who is quite at home on a hillside and climbs like a mountain goat, chattered the whole way up, and for once I let him chatter and forbore to contradict even his most absurd remarks. When, however, he began to make an abstruse calculation as to our relative difficulties in climbing, saying that with so much more weight than he had and so much less muscle, it was therefore so much more difficult for me than for him, I was provoked to give him a breathless but well-directed prod with my umbrella which sent his figures to the winds, and that sum was never finished.

We certainly had a magnificently comprehensive view from the top of the Takht, not only of the town of Srinagar, but the whole valley of Cashmere lay spread before us with its embracing circle of snowy hills. We could trace the windings of the Jhelum too sometimes embosomed in foliage or marked out by lines of poplars and sometimes a mere line of light. The Buddhist temple at the top of the hill was built, some say, before Christ, but others say about the time of the conquest of England. It is small but substantial, and its position makes it imposing. It is now used as a Hindu temple and in the middle of it is a huge, black marble linga with a serpent coiled round it, beside which on his knees was a priest offering milk and flowers and burning incense and singing in a loud harsh chanting tone, 'Siva o, Siva o'. As his lips did not move I could not tell from whence the sound proceeded till I went quite close to him.

The sun, my great enemy in these parts, was appearing as we started on our descent but I had now time and strength to linger and pluck the wild flowers and sweet herbs that clothed the sides of the hill. When nearly at the foot we met a lady and gentleman going up. The lady looked already quite distressed and I felt sorry knowing what was before her. She was dressed in a thick black dress and a veil, and the sun was well up and shone full in her face. I felt very proud and happy to have conquered the Takht and in the flush of victory was wheedled into promising to go up Hari Parbat the next morning. This is a hill in the middle of the city, on the top of which is a fort which looks rather impressive at a distance and which Tom had always desired to visit.

Accordingly we rose as before, I with much internal reluctance, and we went down the river in the most promising manner but when, at about the fourth bridge, our boatmen proceeded to put us ashore, saying that we should now have to walk four miles, I plucked up courage and refused to stir from the boat. Tom walked off alone looking foiled and gloomy, and I proceeded to take a sketch of a very picturesque ziarat on the riverbank that I had often admired. Time flew in this pleasant occupation and in little more than one hour Tom was back again, having found the walk only about a mile each way. He was glad I did not go as it was through the dirt and smells of the city – such dirt and such smells! The fort too was very unsatisfactory, dilapidated mud walls and a few antiquated guns.

Soon after this the English mail arrived and now, having nothing to wait for, we decided to break up our little encampment and to go for a day or two to Lake Manasbal on our way to the Sind Valley, where we had promised to join some friends who were shooting there. So one morning there was a little unusual stir and bustle in our entourage and then we

Riverside Ziarat

'Folded our tents like the Arabs
And silently stole away'.

It really is astonishing how soon encampment vanishes. For weeks perhaps it remains the same and looks quite an established feature in the landscape, when suddenly the place that knew it knows it no more. There has been no noise 'or hideous hum', no sound of wheels or anything to attract attention, perhaps a little more movement than usual as the things were carried away, and then the place which was so lately a centre of busy life is silent and deserted.

We had been very happy in the Ram Munshi Bagh and felt quite sentimental at leaving it. The only drawback to our happiness had been the flies which surrounded us in swarms, attracted no doubt by the ripe mulberries that grew in such profusion. We kept them out of the tents by means of chicks, but they were a terrible nuisance all day long; at meals we were nearly devoured by them, and had to keep a servant continually flapping them off the food. They even followed us as we went down the river and Tom used to wrap his head up in a large pocket handkerchief, thereby making himself look like a portrait of the poet Cowper with his head swathed in linen. This arrangement seemed satisfactory to him - although the flies had still ample liberty to walk over his face - until, at length, he would begin to search about for his pocket handkerchief. I allowed him to rummage as long as I thought good for him, and would then considerately direct his attention to the fact that it was on his head. Life is so placid and uneventful on board a boat that unless we took advantage of the mild amusement offered by each other's peculiarities we might possibly find it dull. Our bhisti's post during these trips is a complete sinecure, but he makes himself useful in various ways helping with the cooking and in pitching tents. Our servants are all Muhammadans and it is now the month of Ramadan when good Muhammadans fast strictly from sunrise to sunset - they do not allow even a drop of water to pass their lips. This is, of course, very painful and trying to them especially when they are travelling all day and have to pitch tents and cook dinner at the end of it, but we try to spare them as much as possible. The khansama, I believe, really fasts and he often looks very worn and jaded towards the end of the day, but the others look so comfortable that I suspect them of taking snacks at convenient intervals, and small blame to them, poor creatures.

By sunset we had reached Lake Manasbal, which is connected with the river by a rather tortuous canal. It is surrounded by mountains and we decided to encamp for a day or two under the shadow of a lofty hill that overhangs the far end of the lake. We chose a spot high up on the mountainside, under a group of fine chenars from between whose branches we had a most perfect view of the lake and the distant mountains. Behind us was a waterfall which was carried artificially round our plateau in two streams, which blended and formed another waterfall below us.

On the first day of our stay here it was stormy. We wrapped up in warm clothes, however, sat in the doorway of our tent and rather enjoyed the wind and rain. Towards afternoon we had the further amusement of watching the proceedings of some new arrivals who were arranging themselves a little below us. As the storm cleared up we went for a long walk round the borders of the lake, following the course of a pretty stream which, instead of being allowed to fall into the lake as it would naturally wish to do, is conveyed round it at a certain height for purposes of irrigation. Mulberries as usual abounded, which we stopped to eat when so disposed. On reaching our tents we found that our neighbours from below had come to call on us. They were very agreeable people so we had a pleasant talk, and as they were old travellers they gave us a good deal of information about our future route. They told us that they had left the encampment of the Nasim Bagh, where we were a few days ago, because it had become so painfully civilized; people had even begun to wear dress coats when going to dine in each other's tents. It certainly is a tendency of modern travellers to take their own life with them instead of accommodating themselves to the life they find. By doing so they miss its peculiar flavour, make their travels more of a toil than a pleasure, and might almost as well stay at home.

The next morning early we took what we thought was a last look at the beautiful view through our leafy screen and were up and away, for we had promised to meet our friends on the next day at the latest. So we had another quietly blissful day in the boat, floating through the most exquisite scenery, reading and writing and calling for food when hungry. Bacon says somewhere that people keep diaries at sea where there is so little to chronicle and neglect to do so on land journeys where there are so many more interesting things to describe. He wonders at this but I do not. At sea there is very little to do, and you are

Lake Manasbal

called upon to make no exertion whatever, and it is the same on our river and lake voyages. We have absolute leisure and so many beautiful and amusing things constantly passing before our eyes that it is quite a temptation to describe them. While in travelling by land it really is impossible to write during the actual journey, and after a harassing march or a hard ride you feel too tired to sit down and write about what you have seen and done, and so the days slip away unrecorded.

We passed on out of Manasbal through water lilies and loveliness into the Sind River, and in the afternoon reached Ganderbal where we received a letter from our friends telling us that they were encamped at Larri, about three miles from the shore. Since the distance was so short we decided to stay and sleep on the river's bank as there was a difficulty in getting coolies at that hour, and our servants looked hungry and woebegone. We soon had our tent pitched and allowed them to go to their food.

CHAPTER 3

The river is not navigable after it enters the Sind Valley so we left our boats in the morning and walked straight off in the direction of the mountains. The man who had been sent by our friends to guide us soon pointed out a group of chenars under which he said they were encamped, but we had to go steadily on for a long time before we came to them. Meanwhile, it was getting hot so we stopped and rested in a cherry orchard and our servants gathered us some cherries. Presently the owner appeared with some milk which, however, turned out to be sour. These people are very dirty and don't trouble to clean their milk vessels so that you can never be sure of the milk being sweet, even though it may be fresh. We paid him for his cherries, after allowing our servants to eat their fill and take away some for tarts.

Soon we reached the spot where our friends had pitched their tents. It was a most pleasant meeting but we could not conceal our astonishment at each other's appearance. Captain L. had grown a beard, and his wife looked much more robust than she did in India. As for us, we had fine red-brown complexions instead of our pasty Indian ones, and being all got up in our oldest clothes we presented an unusual appearance in each other's eyes. We soon had our tents arranged; the group of chenars was large enough to shade us all. They were situated on an elevated spot overlooking the valley, which is very wide here and is full of rice fields. A little stream brawled behind us and immediately beyond it the mountains rose to a considerable height. In the far distance through the outlet of the valley we could still see the Takht-i-Suleiman and Hari Parbat.

We found a great deal to talk about and it was very delightful to gather round a large camp fire after dinner and compare our experiences. On one occasion we had just arranged ourselves, the gentlemen with their cigars still unlighted when, without a moment's warning, a violent storm burst upon us. The blazing logs were blown in all directions, showers of sparks flew straight in our faces, my cap blew far away into the darkness and, when I had recovered it and my equilibrium generally, I was amused by the presence of mind displayed by Mrs. L. and my husband who had each seized a bottle of whisky and their respective glasses which they held tenaciously. Captain L. clung to a lamp, which however was soon blown out. We thought the wind would cease but it blew harder than ever. The fires as well as the lights were soon extinguished, the servants having aided this desirable consummation by pouring water on the logs fearing lest the blazing brands should set the tents on fire. The greatest confusion reigned, our belongings were fluttering about in all directions, and the tents were flapping and straining in the most threatening manner. We thought it best to go out from under the trees for fear of a falling branch. The thunder roared, and each flash of lightning showed a forlorn looking group in the open plain, with caps pulled down and collars turned up, clinging to each other for shelter against the almost overpowering wind. At last the rain drove us in again and, notwithstanding the lightning, we all crouched to leeward of a big tree and waited for the storm to abate. It was quite half an hour, however, before the cigars could be lighted and the fires rekindled, and we then proceeded to solace ourselves for all we had gone through with a little hot whisky and water. We were soon glad to take refuge in our tents, but the storm rose again and raged so in the night that I thought we must be blown away. But we found ourselves all right in the morning.

The trees under which we had encamped had very large trunks and enormous roots. The servants took possession of two, on the branches of which they hung out their clothes and bedding and utilized the hollows for storing away the numerous odds and ends which Indian servants always carry about with them. In the upper branches of one tree was our larder, where half a sheep might be seen hanging above the reach of dogs and leopards, and covered with muslin to keep off the flies. Baskets of cherries and mulberries were stuck in the forks of the trees. Below, a few depressed looking fowls walked about meekly awaiting their last summons.

We sat in the shade of the trees all day working and talking and always feeling ready for our frugal meals. We revelled particularly in this latter sensation for in India, no matter how delicately or temptingly our food is prepared, we have no relish for it, and a feeling of healthy hunger is unknown for months together. We were near enough to Srinagar to be able to send in for letters and for bread, vegetables and other delicacies, and yet we had quite a change of climate. The mornings and evenings in the valley were cool and fresh with a decided nip in the air, and it was never too hot to be out of doors. One little complication arose, however, notwithstanding this halcyon state of things; we found that there was a difference of more than an hour between our friends' watches and our own, which was inconvenient, and with my usual weak desire for compromise I suggested that we should split the difference. The gentlemen smiled in a superior manner and determined to take an observation from the sun, so they put a sheet of newspaper on the ground with a stick through it, and watched the varying length of the shadow. As noon drew near we were all four seated on the ground round the apparatus in a great state of excitement and the shadow was marked every five minutes. Matters grew more and more critical, when an unguarded movement of my umbrella sent the stick flying. We gazed blankly at each other as the shadow disappeared, but my guilty countenance proclaimed me the culprit. The stick was set up again as nearly as possible in its former position, but an element of uncertainty had crept into the calculations, and the masculine love of accuracy could not be satisfied till another day had been devoted to the operation. On the second occasion, I was politely but firmly requested to keep out of the way and, as the crisis approached, my every movement was regarded with apprehension. The result of the calculation proved that we were each half an hour wrong, so that if my despised advice had been taken in the first instance, a great deal of trouble would have been saved; this confirmed my opinion that women intuitively jump to the right conclusion while men laboriously reach the same end.

Captain L. went out shooting every afternoon with varying success, and towards evening the rest of us would take walks exploring the valley in different directions. One evening, on our return, we found a magnificent female leopard that he had just shot. She was scarcely cold and her beautiful limbs were as supple as in life. I am now the happy possessor of two of her claws, which I intend to have made into brooches for my little girls. For two nights afterwards, while we were sitting at dinner under the chenar trees, we distinctly heard the male leopard, who was with the poor beast when she was shot, growling and whining from the hill immediately above us. He had evidently traced her body to our camp, and connected us in some way with his loss. We felt rather creepy, for the sounds showed that he was very near us, and very angry and unhappy. In the morning, however, when they went out for him with a kid as a decoy and various elaborate preparations, he had vanished and was no more seen and heard.

One evening we went down to the valley intending to make our way to the river Sind. We went on and on, our path being crossed continually by the streams which irrigate the valley. Tom was always deputed to run along the banks till he had found a bridge or crossing place, when he beckoned us to join him. Such bridges I certainly never saw; we were thankful if it turned out to be a respectable tree trunk. Generally it was a slight forked branch, which any of us could have lifted, or a few stones placed at irregular and alarming intervals, many of them under water.

Distances are very deceptive in hill countries and though we had set out most confidently we found that we could not reach the river that evening. There being no proper track, we turned back. But now the streams seemed to come in our way more than ever, and the bridges seemed fewer and further off. Soon we began to doubt about the direction

Bridge

of our tents, there were so many groups of chenars. Darkness too was coming on and, as we had quite lost our bearings and had come to a broad stream which there was no means of crossing, we two ladies sat down rather disconsolately and waited while my husband went as far as a village, which we could see in the distance, to enquire our whereabouts. He soon came back with a man who demonstrated to us that we were within ten minutes' walk of our tents, and that there was no necessity whatever to cross the stream that we thought such an insuperable obstacle. We felt rather ashamed of our obfuscated condition, and in a few minutes were safe at home.

About half a mile from us in one direction was a large village called Larri, very prettily situated on the mountainside. It had a handsome new ziarat which looked quite imposing when seen from the valley below. The Cashmere villages, though untidy in details, are very picturesque. The houses are of two stories and have gabled roofs. The lower storey is built of mud or rough stones and is used in winter for stabling the cattle; the upper storey is of pinewood and has galleries and balconies which are often elaborately carved. The roofs are covered with earth on which grows a plentiful crop of grass and woods. I have seen the roofs of some of the temples covered with purple irises. About a mile in another direction was a ruined city that had evidently, in bygone days, been a place of some importance. We could trace the moat which had enclosed it, and in many instances the foundations of the houses were still definitely marked out.

One evening we came to a little hut where they told us shawls were being made. We had to stoop very low to get into it, and found it dark and ill ventilated. Before a loom of very rude construction sat a wretched sickly looking man; he was very obliging, however, and readily showed us how it was worked. The warp is stretched upon the loom and the weft is worked in a stitch at a time by means of spools covered with different coloured threads, which the man takes up apparently at random but evidently, from the result, with order and design. The shawl then in process of manufacture was worth several hundred rupees.

As a rule the women grind the corn in this country, pounding it with heavy sticks in vessels made from logs of wood slightly hollowed, but occasionally in our wandering we came upon a hut built over a rushing stream which turns a large wheel and the millstone above it. We examined one of these places and found the machinery of the rudest and most primitive construction - it looked as if it was the first water wheel that had ever been thought of. However, it answered its purpose admirably as most of the queer arrangements that prevail in this country seem to do. Still, there is a great waste of its natural resources - this strikes one everywhere.

During our walks we came constantly upon trees laden with fruit. The mulberries were delicious and we often refreshed ourselves with them; in fact we nearly always went home with lips and fingers stained black as a consequence of our indulgence. The cherries were rather sour but were very good for cooking. Apricots, apples and walnuts too were very plentiful, but were not quite ripe. The flowering shrubs were very lovely, wild roses and jasmine grew in great profusion and scented the air. There was also a shrub covered with a beautiful peach-coloured blossom which gave quite a purple bloom to many parts of the valley, and the banks of some of the streams were gay with yellow irises. The stream that ran past our encampment was often utilised to carry logs and trunks of trees to the Maharaja's lime kilns. They are piled up on the edge of the stream and are now and then floated down. At one place the stream was full of them, and they lay so still and looked so solid that we felt sure that it would be easy to walk across on them. We incited Tom to try this feat and he started with airy confidence, but when he got to about the fourth log from the shore, it promptly turned over and disappeared. There was a splash, and a struggle and he came scrambling back again, a wetter and a wiser man.

One morning we were seized with a strong desire to go somewhere for a picnic, and finding that Manasbal was only five miles off by land we fixed upon that charming spot as 'the place to spend a happy day'. The two gentlemen walked straight off over the hills, while Mrs L and myself walked about three miles down to the river where we took our boat which was waiting there, and proceeded to do the rest of the journey by water. The way winds charmingly so that we did not reach the lake till twelve, but we had a very pleasant time in the boat, talking and resting and floating past the pretty shores, the only drawback being that we had not a scrap of food, the coolies with the tiffin baskets having gone with our husbands to show them the way. We found ourselves anxiously expected by these two gentlemen. They had spread the cloth under a tree and had arranged the contents of the two baskets with all the care and elegance of which they were capable. After a little while they confessed to having already partaken of a slight repast. We readily forgave them as we had been dreadfully hungry ourselves, and it was only want of opportunity that had prevented us doing the same. Besides, they were quite ready to join us and from the way in which they did justice to the things set before them we should never have imagined they had had anything previously.

We spent a delightful afternoon lying on the grass reading and sleeping. Then we had tea and sent our servants home with the things, we ourselves taking a boat to the other end of the lake as we wanted to visit an old fakir who lives there. He has for many years been making himself a grave inside the mountain. It is a large tunnel, 90 feet long, which he has scooped out in the cliff. We explored it to the end, lighting our way by some matches that we had in our pockets. At the end of it is a shelf on which the old man intends his body to lie; over it is an arch, very highly ornamented. When we came out, the old gentleman told us that from the earth taken from his grave he had built the house in which he lived. 'Here', he said, 'is my house for this life, there is my house for the next. I await the time when God shall call me; God knows best'. He is a fine looking old man with gentle courteous manners. When we left he gave us some baskets of cherries, which attention we returned with a small present.

By this time the sun was sinking towards the horizon and we all started off walking over the hills to Larri. When about half-way there we felt hot and thirsty so we sat down on some logs of wood near a farmhouse and called for milk. Cows quickly appeared, were promptly milked and we drank and went on our way refreshed. After a pleasant but stony and climbing sort of walk, we reached our tents from whence some of us were presently to be heard singing fervently 'Home, sweet home' as we were dressing for dinner.

I would here mention that the way in which we ladies dress for dinner is to put on large warm cloaks, and cloth caps with ears. Captain L. wears an ulster and my husband considers his costume the correct thing when he has donned a dressing gown and a pair of gaiters. These toilets would not be considered suitable under ordinary circumstances, but they are eminently adapted for our dining hall under the stars and the chenars.

On the last evening that we were to be together we opened a bottle of the wine of the country. The Maharaja, by the way, has a wine manufactory on the shores of the Dal Lake that is conducted by Frenchmen and turns out two kinds of wine, one a very good sound claret, the other a sweet kind of Chablis or Sauternes, which also is very palatable. We were drinking each other's healths and making appropriate parting speeches on the above mentioned occasion when we were interrupted by one of the violent storms to which these parts seem to be especially subject. In a moment our congenial party was broken up; we had to rush to our tents, each seizing our respective plates, chased by burning brands from the fire. The servants having got used to these little occurrences soon put out the fire, secured our belongings, and in five minutes we were settled inside our tents finishing our interrupted dinner and, from that distance, shouting our good wishes for the morrow.

Our friends left early on the following day, and we spent some time in arranging our plans for the further exploration of the Sind Valley. As the roads are in many parts very difficult we determined to go in light marching order, and so sent one of our tents and all the luggage we could possibly spare to be stowed on board the boat at Ganderbal. It rained in the evening and we felt rather lonely and bereft, so we dispensed with the camp fire and retired early in preparation for our start the next morning.

We rose at dawn with stern decision but feeling dismal in the extreme, and it was so cold after the rain that I was beguiled into wearing a warm cloth habit which I afterwards bitterly regretted. A decent looking pony was brought by one of the villagers for me to ride and, as the man assured me that a lady had once ridden it two years before, I mounted with tolerable confidence. For a time he went very well till he came to a place where he could see his owner's house on the farther bank of the stream and then, like Horatius, when

'he saw on Palatinus the white porch of his home'

he

'with his harness on his back, plunged headlong in the tide'.

In vain I pulled and shouted - he neighed and defied me. The syce, however, waded in to the rescue and we soon had him on the right road again, and then, after one bout of caracoling and kicking, he made no further protest.

We were now on our way to the Wangat valley, which is an off-shoot from the Sind valley, and which contains the ruins of some fine temples of great antiquity that we were anxious to visit. Our way at first was easy and pleasant and, as we went on, the scenery grew wilder and more lovely. I can scarcely describe the profusion of wild flowers. Whichever way we turned we were surrounded by beauty and luxuriance. The mountains too were very fine and were clothed in verdure from head to foot. Our way was beautifully shady and bowery and I should have enjoyed the ride exceedingly had I not been constantly under the necessity of trying to avoid the fate of Absalom. My hat was several times torn from my head by boughs and once or twice I was nearly dragged off the pony bodily. This was really a great drawback to my pleasure. Besides, my saddle, having been intended for a much larger horse, was loose and kept slipping directly the road was at all steep. After having turned into the Wangat valley and found the path very rough and precipitous, and after several ineffectual efforts to tighten the girths, the saddle finally turned completely round with me and I fell at a very dangerous part of the road. Fortunately, my face was turned inward from the precipice so I lighted on the bank and was not hurt. After this catastrophe I decided to walk as we had no means of tightening the girths; but the sun was very hot and, encumbered as I was with my heavy habit, I was rather unhappy.

At one place there was not the least sign of a path. We had literally to scramble with hands and feet round the face of the cliff, stepping on and holding by little projections which we chose with the greatest care. The pony was dragged round somehow, slipping and slithering over the rocks, with loud shouts from the syce and injunctions to 'Rubhur dar' which means, 'take care'. My husband took what he thought was a better road lower down, but the syce was very unhappy about him and told me a thrilling story of a sahib who had fallen from the lower road two years ago and been killed at once. This did not tend to increase my comfort and confidence as I was crawling along, but at this juncture I caught a glimpse of Tom, who had wisely turned back and was following us.

We reached Wangat at last very weary, and after choosing a place for our tents sat down on the ground to wait for our servants and luggage. As there was a hut near by we called to a man and asked for some milk, but he said the cows and goats were all out for the day and would not be home till night when they came of their own accord. We, however, vehemently urged him to catch something and milk it, as we were famished having started at six o' clock after the slightest possible repast. At last, moved by our entreaties and promises, he went off to see what he could do.

Meanwhile we sat and waited and presently a keen wind arose and it began to rain. We had no shelter but I had our waterproofs on the pommel of my saddle – a most necessary precaution in Cashmere travelling – so we arrayed ourselves in them and sat two hours there, on the bare hillside, a forlorn looking couple under a white umbrella. At last we saw the man approaching with some milk and, hungry and thirsty as we were, it was like nectar to us. The rain too stopped about this time so we sat still and dried ourselves in the sun.

At about two o' clock we were further cheered by the sight of our servants in the distance, wending their way up the hill. Notwithstanding that they must have been about as tired as we were, they soon had a meal ready for us. When our tent was up we both lay down and went to sleep and did not wake till dusk, when we had dinner and immediately went to bed again - I never slept more soundly in my life.

The next morning we were up betimes and, taking our breakfast in a basket, we set off to walk to the ruins, which were about two and a half miles up the valley. Leaving our servants to have a good rest, we took one coolie to carry the basket and show us the way. The valley is about seven miles long and only about five hundred yards wide. It is enclosed by very high granite mountains which are clothed principally with pines, whose sombre foliage is here and there relieved with streaks of vivid green, showing where an avalanche or a granite boulder has cleared a path for itself, sweeping away the pines; in time the bare streak has become overgrown with new foliage. As we went along that morning towards the head of the valley - which is bounded by a magnificent snow-covered peak, round the sides of which flow the mountain torrents which unite and pass roaring down the valley to join the Sind - the air was keen and bracing. Our way lay through pleasant paths on the mountainside, shaded with nut bushes. When we came to an open space it was often covered with rose bushes, the flowers of yesterday having faded from the heat of the sun to almost delicate shell-pink, while those blossoms which had only opened their eyes that morning were often of the deepest crimson. All along our path, too, grew wild strawberries of most delicious flavour, which we continually stopped to gather.

As we were going happily along the coolie, who was in front, suddenly made a great commotion with his stick and a large fat snake rushed across my path into the bushes. I had time to see that it was all yellow and green and brown, and would have been pretty if it had not been a snake. According to my wont on such occasions, I screamed and stood poised on one foot, not knowing which way to flee and expecting to see snakes on all sides of me but, in a minute or so, my sober senses came back and I went on, treading gingerly and trying to comfort myself with the idea that snakes were as much afraid of me as I was of them. Before I lived in snake countries I always thought, probably from highly seasoned books of adventure which I may have read, that the creatures advanced ravening to attack you, that they sprang upon you from trees and from the roofs of houses, that they lay await for you in your bed, and in fact were thoroughly active and aggressive, so that the discovery of the comparatively mild and unobtrusive habits of snakes was a great relief to me.

On reaching the temples we chose a shady spot among the ruins and had our breakfast, quenching our thirst with water from the sacred tank which was close at hand and the water of which was very cold and pure, as it issues from a spring at the foot of the mountains.

This spring is a square kind of reservoir, overshadowed by trees and ferns, and the ground around it is thickly carpeted with grass shoes which have been left there by the pilgrims who visit the place. These shoes are generally worn by Europeans also when climbing the hills as they are supposed to prevent slipping. They have to be worn over a peculiar sort of felt or woollen sock with cloven toes so that the cord which fastens on the shoe may pass between the toes. We have worn them a little but find them very uncomfortable, and therefore only keep them ready for emergencies. We both wear comfortable well-fitting laced boots of yellow unblacked leather, which suit us admirably and seem to be just the thing for this kind of travelling.

There are two temples, one called Nagbal, and the other about 150 yards away called Rujdainbal. They are both built of enormous hewn stones kept in place simply by their own weight. The ground around them is strewn with similar stones in heaps, which shows that they must originally have been buildings of some extent. Their great antiquity is evident from their appearance; large trees are growing out of the roofs and displacing the ruins in every part, and the scenery around is as wild as can be imagined. I took two sketches of the temples; their proportions are very massive and much skill and labour must have been extended in shaping and rearing them. They belong to the period of Nag worship, or the worship of natural objects such as streams, trees, snakes, etc., which it is said Alexander the Great found prevalent when he invaded India.

After staying two or three hours we started on our return; the way was lovely as ever but hotter. However, it was downhill and we reached our tents at about one and found tiffin ready. After resting a little and writing letters, which we hoped to be able to post from Kangan the next day, we were moved towards evening to explore the lower part of the valley. We had to cross the river by two very primitive bridges just where it is divided by an island, one bridge consisting of three slender pine trunks laid across without fastening of any kind, and the other of two pine trunks with rough split logs laid across transversely

Temple

and tied here and there with twigs and bits of bark. I quite lost my nerve at the first one for the span was very wide, and the vibration of the poles was terrible. I had to go over it in the most ignominious manner about an inch at a time, holding by the tail of my husband's coat and for once giving clear evidence of being decidedly the weaker vessel. The river beneath us was a big roaring torrent and gave a terrible idea of restless power, it haunting my dreams in fact all night.

The next morning we allowed our servants to pack up after breakfast, and to go leisurely on to Kangan while we stayed at Wangat to finish our letters under the shade of a tree. In the afternoon we started to follow them, first crossing the river by the terrible bridges, and then going along the other side of the Wangat valley. The bhistie assisted me on this occasion to make the perilous transit, walking backwards over the bridge and holding a stick for me to clutch. The ride was most delightful, the sun being veiled a little by clouds so that we could enjoy the scenery without being roasted. We had a ride of about ten miles to Kangan and when we got there it was very pleasant to find our tent up and everything comfortably arranged. Kangan certainly is a most delightful spot; it is a lovely wooded flowery plain surrounded by magnificent hills arrayed to the very peaks with the richest verdure.

The telegraph passes through the place on its way to Ladakh. The sight of it certainly gave us a very pleasant sensation though its ugly bare poles looked rather incongruous. In Wangat we had felt, even among all its beauty, that we were cut off from the world, but here at Kangan we were once more in touch with our native land, one with our kind.

We were now quite within the Sind valley, just where it begins to narrow. Our intention was to go by daily marches up to Sonamarg, which is at the head of the valley, and perhaps on to the Zoji La Pass that leads into Little Thibet. The valley bottom was at first a mile or two in width. Our path lay over terraces, slopes and flats, through glades shaded by trees of rich and varied foliage, with jasmine, rose and honeysuckle blossoms scenting the air. It passed by villages almost hidden among the thick foliage of walnut trees, the rich pine-wood tints and picturesque gables of the houses harmonizing perfectly with their surroundings. The valley is bounded on both sides by lofty hills from 5000 to 6000 feet high, richly clothed with forests or covered with thick herbage, sometimes broken by cliffs, and crowned with snowy peaks. It is the finest scenery of its kind in Cashmere and, as we moved along, a panorama of marvellous beauty was continually being unfolded to our delighted eyes.

The river Sind, which runs through the valley, is the perfection of a mountain stream. It comes straight from the snows and glaciers, and rushes along with great volume and velocity through the well-defined channel which it has worn for itself. It is a very pretty sight through its whole course, its colour being of a beautiful grey green just like the colour called eau de nil, picked out most delicately with white foam. It is never smooth and quiet but is constantly breaking out into waterfalls and whirlpools, on whose graceful curves my eyes were never tired of resting.

After one night at Kangan we struck our tents very early having before us a march of fourteen miles to Gund. The sun was not likely to peep over the hills for an hour so, as it was bitterly cold, I walked the first four miles. At one place, as I was crossing a stream, one of the stones on which I trod slipped and I went into the water up to my knees and after this, of course, I had to go on walking till I was dry. After about six miles we came up with our canny old bawarchi, who had taken possession of a most delightful little glade where he was busily preparing our breakfast, and after coffee, chops and cherries we felt equal to attempting the remaining eight miles.

The roads are very bad, however, and even in riding it is impossible to go more than two miles an hour, so that we did not reach Gund till noon. The servants and tents did not come up till three hours after us, and I was very tired and cold. We were both thinly clad too and had nothing extra to put on, so we wandered about feeling rather dejected, or sat down on stones or the roots of trees, trying to keep out of the wind. The tents were scarcely up before it began to rain seriously; however, we could now get at our warm clothes so we made ourselves comfortable. The villagers brought us plenty of milk and butter and we also bought a nice little sheep for three rupees with the intention of subsisting on it while in the cold hill districts, and so, for the next week or more, its carcass accompanied us, growing smaller daily.

In the morning the rain had ceased but everything was very wet, and the tents were consequently so heavy that the coolies begged us to stay for some hours while they dried. We did not start therefore till noon, for which we were afterwards very sorry for we found that, in these parts, however fine the morning might be, rain generally comes on soon after noon. Accordingly it rained heavily all the way from Gund to Gagangair, and though it was only nine miles, we were only able to go very slowly, the road being more and more steep and difficult and also terribly slippery from the rain. At one place where there was a rather prosperous looking farmhouse, we stopped and bought some milk and asked for shelter. The man took us into one of the open veranda-like galleries, and spread a numdah on the ground for us to sit upon. A numdah is a rug of thick felt made from the hair of goats or camels, dyed in brilliant and varied colours and often embroidered, universally used in the country. He was evidently pleased at our accepting his hospitality and all his family, besides his sisters and his cousins and aunts, assembled in the buildings on the opposite side of the yard where they gazed at us to their hearts' content.

We stayed half an hour and then went on, hoping that the rain was abating, but it was soon worse than ever and when we arrived at Gagangair it was pelting furiously. Here there was no shelter but a large walnut tree, under which we decided to camp when our tents should arrive. We hailed some men who were near and told them to bring us wood for a fire; we applauded them vigorously as they came dragging big branches to feed the flames that were soon roaring away, notwithstanding that everything was dripping. Oh, how we rejoiced in that fire! It was the solitary bit of comfort in our unhappy lot, for we were wet to the skin, cold and hungry, and had nothing to sit on but wet stones and nothing but a dripping tree to shelter us. We sat shivering in the keen wind, for we were now very near the snows - in some places it looked as if we could reach them in a walk of ten minutes. The smoke from the fire nearly choked us, but at last the servants appeared and after a tin of hot soup we felt warmed and comforted.

When the tent was pitched, however, we were not much better off, for the ground was wet and everything, even the bedding, was damp. I could not get warm all night and slept uneasily. It kept on raining, there was a continuous rumble of thunder among the hills, and the river ran roaring past. Towards morning I was effectually roused by something cold and heavy and lively falling on my face from the roof of the tent. I sat up and shook it off, feeling volumes, but I never knew for certain what it was. Only in the morning I saw a hideous, black, clammy, lizard-like creature run out of one of my boots, and I felt certain from its shape and size that it was the very 'thing' that had fallen flop in my face in the darkness of the night. Truly, 'necessity makes us acquainted with strange bedfellows'.

In the morning we made an early start for Sonamarg in order to escape the rain that, we now knew from experience, might be expected later in the day. From Gagangair the Sind valley narrows considerably. The river flows on one side at the very foot of the mountains, and on the other there is only a very small strip of land between the stream and the opposite hills. Presently, as we went along, the great rocky range on the one side approached the opposite range so nearly that the valley becomes merely a gorge through which the river goes foaming along, while the path is carried among the large fallen boulders that lie at the foot of the steep overhanging cliffs. For some miles it is quite impossible to ride, even on the safest of hill ponies, and it is really far easier to get down and walk. This is said to be the worst bit of road in the whole two hundred and fifty miles from Srinagar to Leh, and I can readily believe it for it would be difficult to imagine anything much worse. I did not object to the walking, however, for it was bitterly cold. We were near the snows and the sun was nearly all day veiled in clouds. We saw some glaciers on the other side of the river and amused ourselves by trying to throw stones into them. Presently we came to a large glacier on our side of the stream which it was necessary to cross. It was all half melted ice and snow and the track was only a few inches wide and very slippery. Sometimes there were big holes in it, underneath which we could see the water rushing and across which we had to stride, trusting for a foot-hold to the soft broken ice at the edges. Our pony had to be taken by another road and I was thankful indeed when

Sonamarg

we got safely across.

After this we emerged from the gorge and the road opened out somewhat. Soon we came to a broad grassy plain two or three hundred feet above the stream, covered with buttercups and forget-me-nots, meadowsweet and many other English flowers. Before us, round the shoulder of a hill, lay Sonamarg or 'Golden Meadow'. It is merely a collection of less than a dozen huts lying in a sheltered corner of the fertile plateau, but its surroundings are wondrously beautiful. The ground is undulating, composed of little dells and hillocks covered with the greenest grass, gay with wild flowers. The lower slopes of the hills are clothed with silver fir, birch, sycamore and other trees of brightest green, above which there rise great masses of bare rocky mountains with snowy peaks and with glaciers lying in their hollows. The verdant green of the grass, the golden buttercups, the vivid blue of the sky and the pure snows all go to form a picture of surpassing loveliness; but if these hues were transferred to canvas they would be criticized most mercilessly as crude and raw and wanting in tone, but seen with the natural eye this purity and brilliance of colour has a most pleasing and exhilarating effect.

We had not long, however, to admire the beauties of the place for scarcely had we arrived than it began to rain in the most uncompromising manner and the people coolly informed us that it generally rained almost daily, in fact, at that part of the year. This accounted for the fresh vivid colours, which we so much admired, and for the spongy soil, which we did not admire, remembering that we should have to pitch our tents on it. We took shelter in one of the huts, sitting down on the floor on some skins and numdahs spread for us, but the place was frightfully dirty and the door was obstructed by the heads and bodies of the inquisitive villagers. As many as could possibly get a view came to look at us, and those outside applied their eyes to the chinks and crannies in the wooden walls, and continued to gaze at us unwinkingly as long as we stayed. They brought us some milk but it was very sour from having been put into dirty vessels, which is a good specimen of their wasteful ways.

Our servants were a long time in coming up, since the tents were so heavy with wet they had been obliged to put on extra coolies, and they could only travel very slowly with their loads over the rough steep roads. So, when we were tired of our rather stuffy shelter and of being the cynosure of neighbouring eyes, we walked about in our dripping waterproofs. When at last they arrived matters were not much improved; the tents were damp and mouldy, the fire would not burn and the dinner was smoky and half-cooked. We could not blame the poor creatures, however, for to cook anything, anyhow, was a merit under such circumstances.

Notwithstanding all this, Tom was enterprising enough to plan an expedition for the

Bridge at Sonamerg

next day, the magnitude of which made my hair stand on end. He determined to go to the Zoji La Pass, which is fourteen miles from Sonamarg and an awful climb, and then contemplated returning the same day. On hearing of this I promptly resolved to spend the day in bed trying to get warm and dry, which ignoble resolution I faithfully carried out.

Tom started at 6 a.m. with a man to show the way and a coolie to carry a basket of food. Meanwhile, I found I had caught a bad feverish cold, which was not surprising after the hardship of the last few days, so I wisely gave myself up to the healing influence of warmth and rest.

We had promised our servants to stay at Sonamarg so that they could celebrate their Eid, which is the feast at the conclusion of Ramadan. They could get nothing to eat, however, even milk was scarce, and the coolies whom we had kept for the journey down could not procure their daily rice. With the constant cold and wet, in addition to this scarcity of food, they were all very unhappy and begged that we would leave Sonamarg as soon as possible and hurry down to Gund, where they were sure of getting plentiful supplies. I readily promised to use my influence but felt doubtful whether Tom would be inclined for an early start the next day after his twenty-eight miles walk. In fact, I was very nervous and unhappy about him, especially as all afternoon it rained steadily.

At about 6 p.m., however, he returned, tired and drenched but as cheery as possible. I gave him some hot tea at once and dinner as soon as he had changed his clothes, and here follows his own account of his adventures:-

'Left Sonamarg at 6 a.m. When we had gone about a quarter of a mile from the tents, the milk in the tiffin basket began to leak and made a milky way down the coolie's back. I did not want the bother and delay of going back again, and 'it's no use crying over split milk', so without more ado I drank it all up, and it must have been about a quart. This may seem philosophic but it was a mistake for, thus gorged and bloated, the journey was more of a burden than it would have been. But the work was before me, so I put on steam and arrived at the half way house, half way to Baltal, at ten minutes past seven after a good swinging walk up hill and down dale.

It is the pace that kills - the milk may have had something to do with it! I thought of Lieutenant Ford and his ruptured heart after climbing the Takht-i-Suleiman, and moderated my pace accordingly, so here I am at Baltal at five minutes to nine, with the threatening snow-capped Zoji La before me.

Baltal is a peculiar place consisting of three cowsheds, or what are like three cowsheds.I took a little sketch of the place as it impressed me (Ed. – no record of this sketch), but it is surrounded with magnificent scenery, which is so grand that I have not attempted to introduce it into my sketch. The snow-topped mountains and glaciers are the best I have yet seen. In the other places we have seen there was snow here and there on the tops of the mountains, but here all the peaks and extensive plateaux are covered with the purest white, so that in places where they catch the light the glare is dazzling.

In marching up the valley towards Baltal, you seem to be coming to the end of everything, but on nearing this end you find the valley takes a turn both to the right and to the left. The Sind comes down from the right, where two marches farther on is Amarnath with its sacred caves and guardian snake; the road to Zoji La is on the left. The flowers here are very beautiful, finer than anything I have ever seen, even at Sonamarg – the Golden Meadow – so I sat down and breakfasted among them.

After a change of clothes, I moved on. In one place near the foot of the range the road crosses a very large collection of boulders, rocks and stones, the existence of which the coolie accounted for by saying 'Baraf se nikal agya' – 'they came so by the ice'. They were evidently a moraine formed by a glacier. Here, opposite, is the most magnificent glacier I have yet seen.

This is a very tough bit of marching, steep and trying. One of the men I brought with me from Sonamarg refused to face the pull up the pass, so I had to leave him behind at Baltal. He was a big fellow who at starting made nothing of the journey; in fact, he boasted that he was accustomed to it 'Roz, roz' – that is, daily. It was as usual 'much cry and little wolf'.

About twelve we came to the top of the hill where there was a pile of stones with a flag on the top. The coolie remarked that sahibs always gave baksheesh on arriving at this spot, and called it the Pir Panjal. I had expected to find myself on the top of a ridge looking down on both sides and asked eagerly for the spot where the sahib Log looked towards Dras in Little Thibet, and could scarcely believe the man when he assured me that this was the place. However, I found he was right, for the road on the Thibet side takes only a very slight incline for the first twenty miles. I stayed here half and hour; there were only two kinds of vegetation, the edelweiss and another something like it. The tiffin had been left behind at Baltal and, as it began to rain, I hurried down again over the bypaths, now so wet and slippery that we had to take care or we might have slid down some thousands of feet and never been heard of again.

Wild rhubarb grew on the hillside, among other things, so I gathered a few sticks and took them home for a tart. I also gathered specimens of about twenty different flowers, some quite familiar but many that I had never seen before. At this time I heard a sound as of thunder and the coolie became quite excited and pointed to one of the distant mountains, shouting, 'Baraf, sahib, baraf" ('Ice, sir, ice') - and sure enough I saw an avalanche falling down the mountain side.'

Notwithstanding Tom's walk of twenty-eight miles the day before, we started early in the morning on our downward journey, the day being bright. The place certainly looked lovely but I knew how dismal it could look and was glad to leave it. On passing over the glacier again we saw a place where, on the previous night, a poor pony had slipped with his burthen - he lay smashed and dead on the rocks below. We came also upon a drove of ponies returning without their loads, and the state of their backs was perfectly sickening. In many, the original skin had almost entirely disappeared and the place of the rope was marked out by a network of festering sores. I turned fiercely to the man in charge and informed him emphatically, pointing out the poor ill-used creatures, that if that was his handiwork, to Gehenna he would go, and in Gehenna he would remain, and my husband, who is a firm believer in retributive providence, further informed him that in that same Gehenna he would be an ill-used, sore-backed baggage pony. He did not seem as much impressed as my own servants did; they looked very much awed and I am afraid imagined that I was pronouncing a curse on him.

When I see animals thus cruelly abused, whose lives seem to be nothing but pain and labour from beginning to end, I take refuge in the hope that the doctrine of the transmigration of souls is true and that these are only wicked men who are now in another form suffering the rewards of their misdeeds and cruelties. The only idea that makes the thought of such misery bearable is that it is not quite undeserved. This doctrine has had myriads of believers in all ages and is still inculcated by the Brahmins, who are the ruling power in Cashmere, the Maharaja being a devout Hindoo. It is said that when Gulab Singh, the grandfather of the present Maharaja, died he was supposed to have been turned into a bee, and in consequence bees were declared sacred and it was forbidden to destroy them. After a time, however, the priests declared that the bee containing the Maharaja's soul had been snapped up by a fish, and the consequence of this was that a decree went forth throughout the length and breadth of the land declaring that it was unlawful to eat fish. (Possibly because of pollution? - certainly, after trying the fish of the Jhelum on two occasions, my husband was made violently ill). This was exceedingly inconvenient as fish is the staple food of the boating population who are all Muhammadans, and who made very merry over the prohibition and doubtless evaded it.

Our camping ground under the walnut tree at Gagangair had been ploughed up in the short interval, so we went a few miles further on so as to be nearer Gund, the goal of our servants' desires. It was difficult to find a dry place so we finally pitched our tents in the middle of the track where it broadened out a little and, as we left early in the morning and no one was likely to pass that way but foot passengers and herds of sheep and bullocks who could easily go round us, I don't think anybody was inconvenienced.

We soon reached Gund the next day. After refreshing ourselves with some milk, we left our servants there to purchase their supplies and went on a few miles ourselves to find a camping place which would be nearer Kangan, as it was getting warmer and we wanted to shorten the next day's march. Going along we saw a great commotion among the birds a little off the road and, turning aside to see the cause, found the carcases of a mare and foal who had been killed by a leopard. There were the marks of his fangs on their throats, and after sucking their blood according to his wont, he had left the bodies to be devoured by the fowls of the air. At our approach, five enormous vultures waddled away and a flock of crows, who had been waiting in an agony of impatience in the trees above, immediately proceeded to enjoy themselves. The vultures were so gorged that they did not attempt to fly and it was really very funny, as well as disgusting, to see them labouring up the mountain side, giving now and then a faint flap with their wings, and looking in the distance like fat old gentlemen with their coat tails gently flapping.

During this march, we got caught in a sharp shower, a perfect torrent that drenched us before we could get into our waterproofs. I dismounted and crouched under a bush, but a man presently showed us the way to an overhanging rock under whose shelter we remained till the storm was over. We could not sit upright, so it was very uncomfortable, and Tom further enlivened the time by describing vividly what would happen if the stone fell upon us. When we started again, we found the ground so terribly slippery that it was quite difficult to keep a footing. Nevertheless, as my saddle was quite wet I preferred to walk. It is at times like these, I daresay, that the grass shoes of the country are so useful. We find however as a rule that our shoes are far more comfortable and answer every purpose.

The next day we were soon at Kangan where we stayed peacefully and wrote letters. On coming down the valley, we had been much interested in observing the effect of the varying temperature on the growth of the fruits and flowers. Beyond Gagangair the strawberry plants were only in blossom, between that place and Gund they were ripe in great profusion, and after that they had quite gone off. The apricots and other fruits were scarcely formed high up in the valley, while at Kangan we found them ripe.

We did not leave Kangan till late in the afternoon. Scarcely realizing the difference in the temperature now that we were nearing Srinagar, we had, in consequence, a terribly hot march along the sunny side of the valley, which in this part is planted thick with fruit trees, principally apricots, under whose shade we now and then rested, and ate some of the delicious fruit. It was small, but had the true apricot flavour, and in a week or so will be even riper and more delicious. We were thankful indeed to reach the boat at Ganderbal where we had dinner, and as our lamp was broken and we found it difficult to keep the candle alight on account of the wind, we soon went to bed. What a refuge bed is!

I think the boatmen did a little work in the night for in the morning we found ourselves at Shadipur, and the day was spent in going slowly up the river to Srinagar. The voyage was as interesting as ever. The people in Srinagar are certainly in many ways far in advance of the villagers; they are brighter and more wholesome looking. In the villages I never once saw white clothes of any kind. The people invariably wore the filthy drab woollen garment with the dirty skull cap, which looked as if they had been born in it. Their skins too have a dull lack-lustre look, as if they never washed, and though we were in the Sind valley for nearly a month, and always on the course of the river, I never saw either man, woman or child in the act of washing; whereas here in Srinagar the river bank is alive all day long with people performing their ablutions.

On reaching Srinagar, we decided to go into a bungalow for a few days, as it was too hot to stay in tents. We could now get good bread, fruit and all sorts of little delicacies, and we gave our clothes to the dhobie to be properly washed. During our peregrinations our bhistie had performed the office of washerman in a somewhat perfunctory manner, but we could get nothing ironed or starched. It was really a great pleasure to be in a house again. The rooms of our little bungalow – for which we paid the Maharaja's agent one rupee a day – were matted and covered with dhurries, and when we had arranged our scanty tent furniture to the best advantage, the place really looked quite sumptuous to our unaccustomed eyes.

These bungalows are very roughly built but they are distinguished from almost all other buildings in Srinagar, except the palace, by having small glass windows. In the middle of our bedroom was the trunk of a tree with the bark scraped off, which supported the roof. Six headless nails were stuck in this post at about six feet from the floor, and on these I was expected to hang my modest wardrobe. The roof is made of beams of pinewood and at about every few inches, where the beams join, are little cross pieces of wood carved most elaborately. If, instead of taking the trouble to carve these hundreds of pieces, which are of no use and are scarcely seen, the builders had taken the same trouble with the actual edifice, a respectable house would have been the result. This seems to me to be an illustration of the way in which the country is governed. Great stress is laid on all sorts of minutiae, which are of little importance, and the broad principles of good government are totally overlooked.

After one day of peace and rest, my energetic husband decided to start for Gulmarg, taking a tent and two servants. I implored to be allowed to remain behind to recuperate. For a time, camp life is very interesting but it has its drawbacks. After a time it becomes wearisome to be roused daily at early dawn, to have to pack your kiltas, and to have to swallow your chota haziri when you are not in the least inclined for it, and then to have to ride over rough fatiguing roads till noon when you have to sit about on stones or under trees like a snail that has lost its shell, till your tents come up and are pitched. This is seldom satisfactorily done much before evening, and then you are so tired that you are glad to have dinner and go to bed. This, however, is only a one-sided description. The lovely scenery, the bracing air, the way in which you enjoy your meals when you do get them, the amusing adventures you meet with, the brilliant contrivances you evolve which give you a great opinion of your own ingenuity, the thorough change, in fact, from your usual mode of life, give a charm to camp life which can scarcely be described.

I spent the four days of my husband's absence in strict retirement, only exchanging a few remarks with the servant who served my meals. I read, wrote, thought, sewed, sketched and in short bathed

'my weary soul in seas of heavenly rest',

till I began to look forward to another spell of camp life with pleasure. Just when I was beginning to get tired of my loneliness, a day before I expected him, Tom reappeared upon the scene. He had not stayed long at Gulmarg and I shall, as before, allow him to tell his own tale, (with my remarks in parentheses), especially as some of his remarks are in a style which it would scarcely become me to endorse.

> *'Left Srinagar about 7 a.m. by boat for Sopor en route for Gulmarg. Liz (that's me) would bother me to take a lot of things that I didn't want, such as apricots, jam, etc., (how like a man!), so that I forgot one important item which I certainly did want, namely my leather bag with all my belongings. I had gone more than a mile down the river before I missed this indispensable article and then I sent my Fidus Achates, Abdul Rub the khansama, to run and fetch it as fast as his legs could carry him. This was not very fast. However, half an hour passed and he did not reappear whereupon I dispatched a boatman, but remembering that they would only detain instead of hastening each other, I called him back and went myself. All this took some time and consequently was not a good start.*
>
> *In the Wular Lake there were water lilies in profusion with enough of the yellow kind to give variety; and here and there, though early in the season, was a pink lotus, large and lovely, though not yet its full size. It is not difficult to believe that this beautiful flower, has, among other natural objects, had its share of worship for centuries, and that it becomes, in the mind of the pious Hindoo, the throne of the lotus-born Lakshmi. The lotus flower is held by him to be, and well it may be, the emblem of that other divine object - woman's beauty.*
>
> *But these musings are roughly driven to the four winds (and a very good thing too, I think).*

A storm has come upon us suddenly without a minute's notice, and the boat people are now roused to their utmost exertions to punt us to the nearest shore. However, we reach Sopor with the loss of only a teaspoon and a pocket handkerchief, but instead of arriving at noon it was dark when we got into the creek, so I had my tent pitched and slept on shore.

The next day I marched to Babamirishi, a Muhammadan village in a hollow of the hills. It consists of about a dozen houses round a ziarat. Finding a vacant hut I slept in it, the only Christian amongst all these Musulmans. They are not a bad lot; it is impossible to see them obeying the summons of the blind muezzin from the moonlit minaret - 'Come to prayer; prayer is better than sleep; Allah is great; there is no God but Allah; in his hand is blessing; He is almighty' - or bowing down absorbed in their devotions at the setting of the sun, without believing that they are praying sincerely, with entire submission of body and soul to the Great God and to the Faith.

After leaving Babamirishi, the pull up the remainder of the hill to Gulmarg is steep, but not so bad as much that we have met with in other parts of our tour. At last we emerge from the wooded steep into an open glade flanked by low hills covered with pines. Flocks of sheep grazed in the hollows and at the further end a brook rippled over its stony course. It is indeed a most charming spot; the scenery may not be as large as that in other parts of the valley, but it is more lovely, and above all it is peaceful and composing. The soft green sward of the valley, the secluded walks thickly carpeted with pine needles in the neighbouring groves, the mossy banks covered with forget-me-nots, give a charm to Gulmarg that singles it out even in Cashmere, and makes it worthy of its name, 'the Meadow of Roses'.

There were singing birds too, making the woods vocal on every hand, the lark, thrush, cuckoo and the bulbul or Indian nightingale. It seems to me a peculiarly apt place for 'happy lovers'. Given the young men and the maidens, with such surroundings and accessories, proposals must be inevitable. The effect of such scenery, sights and sounds is most tranquilising and brings one under that influence of which Hartley Coleridge speaks: -

'With tender ministrations Thou, O Nature
Healest thy wandering and distracted child,
Thou pourest on him thy soft influences,
Thy sunny hues, fair forms, and breathing sweets,
The melody of woods and winds and waters,
Till he relent and can no more endure
To be a jarring and dissonant thing
Amidst the general voice and minstrelsy.
…………… Healed and harmonized
By thy benignant touch of love and mercy'.

CHAPTER 4

After my husband's return from Gulmarg we spent four days in Srinagar winding up our affairs. We bought fresh stores, paid all our bills, wrote and posted our last batch of letters. The last three days of our stay were cheered by the presence of some friends of whom we had heard at intervals but up to that time had missed. One evening, as I was with Tom on the river sketching, these friends passed us in their boat. After a lively greeting we hurried home, had tents pitched for them, and made arrangements so that we could all be together during the rest of our stay. Afterwards, they resolved to go with us to Islamabad and towards the Liddar valley.

During these few days we were very busy. The tradesmen of Srinagar were as troublesome as ever - they swarmed about us wherever we went, and even in our own house we were not free from them. Whenever we appeared at a door or window we were greeted with 'Salaam Sahib' in half a dozen different keys, and at the least symptom of relenting found ourselves surrounded by silversmiths, enamellers, papier mâché makers, leather sellers, basket makers, men with skins, each holding up a favourable specimen of his work in a most enticing manner. There was no use in looking stern and forbidding, and telling them we didn't want anything - they would reply in the most soothing and insinuating manner 'only look Mem Sahib, no buy'. And if we changed our ground and said we had no time to look at anything they would answer pleasantly 'All right Mem Sahib, tomorrow will come', and sure enough so they did, more amiable and engaging than ever. There is one man, Hamid Jan, a dealer in blue and gold enamel, who amused us very much. He was very handsome, had grey eyes and spoke English rather well. He often came to see us and evidently looked upon my husband as a very funny person and observed all he did and said with great interest. We were one day looking at his wares and as I took a little compass from Tom's hand I observed that the needle had stuck, so I looked at him reprovingly and said, 'You have been doing something to this'. 'Yes Mem Sahib' says Hamid Jan eagerly, 'he been knocking it gainst the chair like this, like this, I saw him'. I could not help laughing for he seemed just like one boy telling of another.

These Cashmeris have a very naïve way of asking for all sorts of little things of English manufacture on which they evidently set great value, such as soap, scent, pins, matches, paper. The latter they paste over their open lattice windows to keep out the cold in winter. In going up the river we often saw handsome new houses with beautifully carved doors and windows, the lattices of which were covered with old newspapers, with here and there a sheet of yellow or pink paper which the owners thought added greatly to the effect.

Our final interview with Sunnund Shah, our benevolent banker, was rather amusing. He asked, as all these people do, for a written recommendation and my husband, according to his custom in such matters, wrote a couple of lines, short and to the point. Sunnund however was not satisfied. He looked at the meagre testimonial gravely and doubtfully, and then said impressively: 'Sahib, from **little** Sahibs I take **little** chitties, but from **great** Sahibs I want **great** chitties'. But even this delicate flattery failed to move Tom to add another word, so with my usual urbanity I took the pen and proceeded to expatiate upon the merits of Sunnund Shah's goods and the cleanliness of his shop, happening to remark in doing so that it was much cleaner and pleasanter to visit than that of Budradeen, one of his rivals, the entrance to whose shop we had found very dirty. This statement of mine caused the greatest excitement in the house of Sunnund Shah. The four brothers crowded round me and with one voice begged me to write it, my disapproval of Budradeen' s shop, one of them adding eagerly 'Write that it smell, write that it smell'.

One fine morning we said a final adieu to the beautiful, quaint, picturesque, dirty city,

Pampur

whose like we shall never see again, and sailed with our friends up the river towards Islamabad, our flotilla consisting of five boats containing ourselves and about twenty boatmen and servants. The river above Srinagar is much prettier and pleasanter than the part below it. It winds very much and we seldom had a stretch of more than a few hundred yards before us. But each bend opened out new varieties and combinations which, though compared with the wild beauty and magnificence of the Sind Valley might be considered tame, yet gave us great pleasure from their comparatively English character.

The first night we stopped at Pampur, a small village where the most striking object is a ziarat. There is also a summer palace belonging to the Maharaja. It is a large building round a courtyard; the rooms are bare but the doors, windows and ceilings are of pinewood, handsomely carved in different patterns. The women's apartments were in a rather remote corner of the place and we noticed that they were not so well kept and arranged as the other parts of the house. The latticework of the windows too was built up so that it was impossible for them to look over it, and they could only peep through without being seen.

We dined under a group of fine chenars and then the gentlemen retired to their tents, but Mrs. M. and I preferred sleeping in our boats thinking that we should be the sooner ready to start in the morning.

On our way up the river the next day we stopped to examine the ruins of some temples at Avantipur. These are mere heaps of massive stones without much form or connection, but here and there the ornamentation of a pillar or an archway may be traced, showing that the details must have been very fine. At one corner a part had been excavated, and here the form of the building was better preserved. There were two or three perfect trefoil arches with their pillars and pediments, and here and there the remains of what looked like gargoyles could be distinctly seen - one indeed was remarkably like the winged head of a cherub such as we see in more modern temples.

We landed in the evening at a place called Sorsoo, and after dinner passed an hour or two in singing in the moonlight, some of us developing unexpected talent. The next day we continued our voyage. Just where the river was very broad we saw two snakes swimming across - we could trace them the whole way as their heads were held above water for breathing purposes. Presently, we came to a large new-looking Hindoo temple on the bank of the river, opposite Bijbehara. The temple itself was not interesting, but around it and incorporated in it were some magnificent pieces of Hindoo sculpture, evidently taken from temples of very ancient date. They were principally of black marble. One was a very handsome and elaborate sculpture of Krishna and Garuda, and another of a Brahmin bull; these two had little pavilions built over them. The elephant-headed Ganesha also figured largely and there were several colossal lingas. Built into the new walls were fragments of old stone, sculptured with representations of incidents in Hindoo mythology. Some of these were specimens relating to the old Nag, or snake worship.

After landing and looking at this interesting place, we pursued our peaceful way to Islamabad, or rather to Khanabal, which was as far as the boat could go. There we found the horse that had helped so materially to make my journey up from Murree easy and agreeable. It had been sent to await us by our kind friend Janki Pershad. Here too we separated our superfluous luggage and gave it in charge of the kotwal *(headman/police chief)* to be sent on to meet us at Shupiyon, which place was two marches on our homeward route towards the Pir Panjal Pass. Meanwhile, after seeing Islamabad, we intended to go with our friends a little way into the Liddar valley, to visit Vernag, the source of the Jhelum, and other places, and then to strike across country into our homeward route at Shupiyon.

The kotwal at Khanabal was a man of mark. He had a large book of chitties, dating from before the Mutiny, of which he was intensely proud. He was tall, his demeanour was imposing, and his voice was deep and loud. The coolies trembled at his nod, and altogether he was particularly capable and well disposed. Having completed our arrangements for the morrow we walked to Islamabad, which was about a mile away. The road was bordered by an avenue of young poplars which will be a feature in the landscape in the time of our grandchildren, but at present look very crude. I cannot say that I admire these poplar avenues much; they are neither graceful nor imposing, though they are certainly peculiar.

Islamabad was a much cleaner town than Srinagar. First we went to see the anail-nag *(sulphur spring)*, which came gushing out of the rock evidently strongly impregnated with sulphur and iron. The smell of the former was very strong and the rocks were red with iron. Then we went down a long stony street, high in the middle, and sloping on both sides into gutters. Its construction kept it dry and clean but made it very difficult and uncomfortable to walk on. This led us to the Sirkari Bagh where there is a residence belonging to the Maharaja, and also some sacred tanks. The springs which supply them issue mainly from a conical hill which overlooks the town. The water is conducted through a series of canals to the garden, where it falls to the ground in a rather fine cascade, and subsides into the tanks, which are about three feet deep, lined with stone and filled with tame fish that are regularly fed and considered very sacred by the Hindoos. The water seemed literally alive with these fishes, and they followed us about for food, crowding over each other in their eagerness. After going through a very neglected garden full of apricot and quince trees, we sauntered back slowly to dinner.

The bungalow at Khanabal was very neglected and dirty; tall weeds were growing up through its earthy floor. But there were rough pieces of wood which bore a slight resemblance to pegs sticking out of the walls here and there, and Tom was so delighted with this unwonted convenience that he hung some article of his raiment on each, till in the dim light I felt as if I was surrounded by Bluebeard's headless wives. However, we were tired with our stroll about Islamabad and soon slept as well as if we had 'dwelt in marble halls'.

The next day was Sunday so we took a short march of six miles (less than a Sabbath's day journey) to Bawan. The road being easy, we all cantered along in great spirits, I on my old friend 'Greatheart' and Tom on a small stout pony of whose prowess he was always boasting but whose appearance caused us a good deal of amusement whenever we could get him in front of us. Though early, it was very hot and we were glad to reach the delicious shade of the magnificent group of chenars that adorn the camping ground at this place. Streams of water rippled and sparkled on every side of us and at first we revelled in the cool shade and the soothing murmur, but as the sun rose higher in the heavens we found it hot and close. A huge mountain immediately above us shut out the breeze, and the trees enclosed us round on every hand.

Near us was another temple with its sacred tank full, as usual, of fishes. We fed them with popcorn and they seemed perfectly ravenous. It would have been easy to catch handfuls of them as they literally tumbled over each other in their eagerness for food. We even put grains of corn into their gaping mouths with our fingers, and they seemed inclined to swallow fingers and all. In the evening we went to see the caves for which the place is celebrated. One has a very narrow entrance high up in the face of the rock; after first stooping and then crawling a certain distance you can stand up and look about you, as it widens out considerably. There is not much to see however. Another large natural cave has been utilized as a temple. The entrance has been enclosed with a door, and at the back of the cave a large shrine has been built. The stones are ponderous but there is but little architectural beauty or finish about it. From the top of the steps leading to this cave, which is very high up in the face of the rock, we had a fine view of the Liddar Valley and river.

The river is pretty here, but it is of an ordinary colour, and does not in any way come up to the beautiful, wayward, graceful Sind which is the prettiest river both in colour and in expression that I have ever seen, or hope to see. In the evening a storm of wind came on, which freshened the air a little but it was a close, stuffy night and we were glad to leave Bawan, notwithstanding the pleasant refreshing welcome it had given us.

Early in the morning the whole cavalcade of us started for Achchibal, intending to stop at Martand, the temple of the sun, on the way. The ruins here are very fine and impressive, standing as they do in solitary and massive grandeur at the foot of the mountains, on an elevated plateau overlooking the valley. The temple, which was probably built and dedicated to the worship of the sun about A.D. 500, consists of a massive entrance gateway in good preservation, leading into a large quadrangle whose dimensions can be easily distinguished. In many places the fluted pillars with the trefoiled recesses between are quite perfect. In the centre is the temple proper, a lofty edifice with two detached wings. The proportions are fine, but its details are not so beautiful and elaborate as those of the temple at Avantipur. It is composed of immense masses of stone, and it is difficult to imagine how they were ever raised to their present position. I took a sketch of the place as it stands without a tree or a house near it, and then we found a place in the shade of the ruins where we sat down and ate our breakfast, which we had brought with us.

After this we rode on through a very pretty and cultivated valley to Achchibal. The

Temple of the Sun, Martand

fields were disfigured by the bleached skulls of cows, goats and other animals, stuck up on poles here and there as scarecrows; they looked very horrible, probably more so to me than to the birds. They reminded me of the American scarecrow which was advertised as being so terrible that it not only kept the crows from stealing but frightened them into bringing back what they had previously stolen.

On reaching Achchibal we found the bungalow - intended for travellers - extremely wretched and dirty, but close by was a lovely garden with numerous pavilions and a handsome substantial pleasure house belonging to the Maharaja, which was particularly clean and in good order as the Resident had been staying there only a few days before. We accordingly took possession of several rooms on the upper floor where it was cool and breezy, and had our beds arranged for the night. The garden was well tended and was full of fruit trees; it was very pleasant to wander about at our own sweet wills, eating apricots and plums. Here, from a cavity at the foot of the mountain, rushes out a large perennial stream, which is supposed to be the long hidden river Bring that has disappeared suddenly on the opposite side of the mountain. About five tons of water a minute are said to rush out from the rock and, after being conducted over the garden in all directions by numerous artificial channels so that you have to be continually crossing bridges, emerge from under the garden wall divided into several waterfalls, which spread out into streams all over the valley. There is a terrace with ruined arches at the foot of the rock, and we climbed up through the broken roof by the help of some friendly roots and, when at the top, found some delicious apricots and raspberries. While gathering them, however, we had to be careful of our footing, as everywhere there were enormous holes in the ruins concealed by the vegetation.

This garden, with its pavilions and streams and fountains, forms a very pretty picture at the foot of the mountain. There is here a very good tekadar, who set the fountains going for our amusement, and made himself agreeable in many ways. On one side of the garden, separate from the pleasure house, was a large building that proved to be the zenana, or women's apartments. It was simply a quadrangle with all the windows looking into a courtyard; the rooms were small but numerous and had evidently at one time been handsomely coloured. The bathrooms had a small marble tank in the middle of the floor to which you descended by steps; these were in very good preservation.

When going to bed at night, we were startled by a loud crashing noise and found that a fine chenar had fallen, but fortunately no one was near to be hurt by it. A few nights previously all the Resident's servants were sleeping under that very tree.

From Achchibal the next day we went to Vernag, which is the source of the Jhelum. It was a long ride of sixteen miles but the road was moderately level for the first ten miles. We then came to a very stiff hill, which tried our horses severely, and upon getting to the top of it we took pity on the poor animals and all dismounted, resolving to walk down the other side, being encouraged to this merciful decision by the steepness of the descent which would have made it both difficult and dangerous to ride. The two gentlemen led their steeds, but Mrs. M. and I, having our habits to hold up, decided to drive ours down the narrow rocky path. It was our first experiment in cattle driving and did not prove very successful, as one or other of the animals kept turning aside to graze on the delicious grass which grew on the mountain side; it took a good deal of coaxing with a stick sometimes to bring them back into the right path. I am sorry to say our male protectors did not afford us the slightest assistance, pretending to be absorbed in the care of their own horses.

At last, weary and wayworn, we reached Vernag, which is a most lovely and picturesque spot, and when we caught sight of another large pleasure house belonging to the Maharaja, our spirits rose at the sight. But alas we found that some English tourists had already taken possession of it, and that they had allowed their servants to scatter themselves all over the place, and had rendered almost every room quite uninhabitable. There was one room, however, in which we two ladies thought we could manage to sleep though it was scandalously dirty. As Mr. M. had a small tent for himself, the amiable Tom had his bed placed outside our door in a large veranda, the other end of which was partitioned off with a sheet by the people who were in possession when we arrived. Unfortunately, the only place where he could put the candle and keep it from being blown out by the wind was in a niche immediately behind his bed, so that while he was undressing his shadow was projected vividly on the sheet, giving a lively magic lantern entertainment to the people on the other side. When I went to bid him good-night I found him very unhappy about this, sitting on the edge of his bed and furtively abstracting one limb after another from his various articles of clothing, but I assured him confidently that the people on the other side of the sheet were asleep, and I can only hope that they were.

We stayed two days at Vernag as it was very cool and shady. Most of the time was spent in lounge chairs under the trees, reading, talking and dozing; it was a perfect realization of dolce far niente. Our surroundings were very beautiful. At the foot of a magnificent mountain clothed with verdure was a large octagonal tank surrounded by a massive arched colonnade of masonry. This is the source of the Jhelum whose course we have traced for so many miles, from Dewal, in fact, the first march out of Murree. The tank seems to lie still and silent under the shadow of the mountain. Its outlet is under the arched gateway of the pleasure house and the water flows on smoothly between walls of masonry under two pretty pavilions, which are built on bridges across it, till it suddenly falls over a rock into the valley below. It is only then that one gains any idea of the vast volume of water that must be constantly and silently upspringing from the heart of the mountain.

The tank is a hundred feet wide and is said to be fifty feet deep, and I should not wonder at all if this is true, for the water is most darkly, deeply, beautifully blue, or rather green. In fact, its colour is most vivid and peculiar; no painter could do justice to it, but I think a brilliant transparent peacock blue would express it most nearly. It is of a wonderful clearness too, and the myriads of fish that inhabit it can be seen as easily as if they were in a glass bowl. We often amused ourselves with feeding them, and wherever we went they followed us in crowds. They would chase a crust of bread all over the lake, and their struggles to gain possession of it were most entertaining. There were so many of them that I could not help suspecting them of being cannibals - they really must prey upon each other. I caught one in my hand with ease, but it felt so queer and slippery that I weakly let it go with a scream.

There are two slabs of black marble in the wall which surrounded the tank, with Persian inscriptions - one stating that the garden was laid out and the spring enclosed by the Emperor Jahangir (who must have been much attached to the spot for during his last moments he asked to be carried to Vernag), and the other giving the names of distinguished travellers who have visited the place, amongst whom was the Emperor Akbar. My husband, being only a schoolmaster, could not of course translate these inscriptions, so we had recourse to our old bawarchi who enjoys the proud distinction of being the only one of our party who can read both Persian and Hindi writing.

On our last evening we had a little farewell feast and a lamb had been bought for the occasion. Our friends and ourselves were going in different directions the next morning, they to Islamabad and Srinagar en route for Gulmarg, and we to Shupiyon on our way towards the Pir Panjal Pass, over which lay our road back to Hindustan.

In the morning we were up before dawn preparing to start, and as the east began to glow with its coming, I could not help, even among all the stir and bustle, apostrophizing in Byron's beautiful words: -

'The morn, the smiling morn!
With breath all incense, and with cheeks all bloom,
Laughing the clouds away with playful scorn,
And living, as if earth contained no tomb.'

After a hurried breakfast and a cordial exchange of good-byes with our friends, and hopes for a happy meeting in Lucknow, we were soon well on our way before sunrise. The road was tedious and uninteresting along little raised paths between rice fields which were so broken and tortuous that we could only go at a foot pace. Our intention was to take a good long march of fourteen miles, but about half-way we found that our servants had stopped and arranged themselves at a place called Chiroot.

It was a good camping ground but we were anxious to get on, not having a day to spare, so after breakfasting under some fine walnut trees we ordered the coolies to take up their loads and go on about seven miles further. After this the road became pleasanter; it was lined with orchards, and people were gathering the apricots in huge baskets. We too, as well as our servants, stopped and gathered apricots and apples whenever we pleased. After a long, weary march we neared a place called Kulgam, and just before reaching it we had to cross a river at least fifty yards wide. The current was not very strong, however, and, as the syce plunged boldly in, I followed him, and by riding carefully managed to get across all right. Tom, however, on his short-legged pony did not fare well; no matter how high he tucked up his feet, he could not keep them out of the water, and occasionally his ejaculations were both deep and loud as the pony stumbled into a hole and nearly disappeared altogether.

The distant view of Kulgam is very pretty; it is on a hill and has two striking ziarats of the form that prevails in Cashmere. We soon found a nice camping ground under two chenars - it was a raised platform with the river running past at a little distance. Cashmere is truly like a well-watered garden - we have never been out of sight and sound of running water since we first entered the valley.

My husband had been ill and feverish all day and the long march through the steamy valley had not made him feel better. Our khansama also, when he came up in the evening, complained of fever and asked for medicine. We, however, determined to push on the next day if possible to Shupiyon, as Kulgam was a very out of the way place, quite off the route and not even mentioned in the guide books. Meanwhile, as our baggage did not come up till evening, we could neither read nor write, but as we always take the precaution to send the cook and his appurtenances on well in front, we had plenty to eat and took no harm. We amused ourselves by watching a colony of herons that had their nests near us. Tom wanted dreadfully to shoot them, but the Maharaja has made a law that herons are not to be shot in Cashmere - and besides, he had no gun so the herons were in no immediate danger! We watched a hoopoe rummaging in the ant-hills with his long slender beak. It looked a most suitable instrument with which to fish out fat ants, but we idly wondered if he did not find it in his way at times, it was so very long and thin - but then we remembered that he was born with it and had probably got used to it.

We saw a great many dogs of sorts at this place. One, a big yellow pariah, came while we were at tiffin and sat down with an air of lively expectation. We threw cold water on him literally and figuratively and he retired for the time, but at dinner, under cover of the dim light, he approached again. He eyed our leg of mutton with such evident intention that I seized the dish and shouted for someone to come and drive him away. A good big stone, well aimed, quenched his ardour for the time being, but in the morning he returned and triumphantly carried off a loaf of bread from under my very eyes. I saw him coming and shouted and gesticulated, making myself look as terrible and ferocious as I could, but as no one else was near, and it was only me, with a look of meek determination, he took the bread and vanished.

We were evidently quite off the beaten road at Kulgam. The people were greatly interested in us, especially the youth of both sexes, who collected in crowds to observe us, as we sat under a tree waiting for our tents. But, whenever my husband put up his eyeglass to look at them, he had no sooner fixed them 'with his glittering eye' than, instead of standing still spellbound, like the Wedding Guest, they turned and fled, tumbling over one another in their flight. The attraction was so strong, however, that they kept returning and after a time, finding that no harm came of it, they stood their ground. However, to the last, a look of awe would come over the face of the bravest of them when the eyeglass was raised, and at one place a man who was ploughing, at the sight of this basilisk function fixed upon him, left his bullocks and plough and fled at the top of his speed, evidently in great fear.

The road from Kulgam to Shupiyon was very long and wearisome. It seemed to us quite twenty miles, and it must have been at least eighteen from the time it took us. At first it lay through rice fields, and the narrow winding paths, raised above the level of the marshy fields on either hand, were very tiresome and fatiguing both for men and horses. Then we came to a part of the valley which was covered for miles with large round stones, evidently worn by the action of water. Indeed, I think that people, who had never heard that Cashmere was originally a lake, could not fail to be struck with the many indications of that fact which abound, especially in these parts. It had a most desolate appearance, there being scarcely any vegetation, and it was all like the stony bed or basin of a lake, with the dregs of a streamlet wandering through it here and there. While bounding it at the foot of the mountains were beach-like terraces or plateaux, looking as if they must at one time have formed the shores of the lake.

During this journey we had to cross innumerable bridges, principally over the streams which irrigate the rice fields; these were most insecure constructions of sticks and earth. Tom's pony went plump through one, with much noise and splashing, and presently my horse failed under me in a most unaccountable manner, and I found that his hind legs had gone through a bridge. He managed to scramble out, however, very muddy but not much damaged. We saw some new wild flowers, a pretty white blossom that grows close to the ground in the stoniest places, just like a garden pink run wild; also a large star-like flower of the most delicate lavender colour. There is a great deal of a scrubby kind of bush here which bears a profusion of peach-coloured blooms and looks in the distance very much like heather. In the Sind Valley this shrub grew to a much greater height and the blossom was very fine, but here the climate is much drier and the soil not nearly so rich.

At last we got to Shupiyon, which is rather a large, lively town for these parts, but the dak bungalow was wretched and dirty in the extreme. We had our tiffin under a tree, but after a time we were glad of the shelter of one of the rooms such as it was, for the enclosure round the building was very dirty and noisy. Groups of men lounged about all day, gambling and quarrelling, horses, mules, cows, and goats added to the dirt and confusion. There was no view whatever, and but little shade. We strolled out in the evening but the air was close and steamy, and we found no road or path of any kind that looked inviting. My husband and the khansama both continued invalidish. The last two tedious marches through the hot unhealthy valley had tried us all very much but, fortunately, the sun had been veiled by a light haze, or we should have felt the heat terribly. On the next march we hoped to get up higher, and as, on the following one, we should have to cross the Pir Panjal Pass, we knew there was some severe climbing before us.

At this juncture our bhistie, whom we had hired at Murree and who had hitherto, so far as we were concerned, pretty well answered the end for which he was created, came and intimated that he did not wish to go with us over the Pass, as it would be cold and difficult. We had provided him with a warm coat for this very journey but we found that, during a little holiday which we had given him, he had with great forethought left it at his village, so that he had evidently never intended to cross the Pass with us. We therefore paid him what was strictly due, but sternly refused him a chitty and left him looking very dejected, but he had behaved badly, and taken a mean advantage of us.

We made an early start for Hirpur, leaving Shupiyon without any regret. The road at first was terribly stony, like that on the other side of Shupiyon, but after two or three miles it became easier. The scenery improved too and everybody felt better. We cantered through the sunny glades and rested in the shade, waiting for our syces to come up. The ground was covered with grass and flowers. One plant struck us particularly; it was just like a strawberry plant and bore a large crimson blossom instead of a white one, but the servants assured us that it never bore fruit. Towards the end of the march the road became precipitous and we saw again the kind of vegetation – ferns, pines, etc. – that had so much delighted us when we came into Cashmere from Murree. The air too was keen and fresh, quite different from the moist feverish climate through which we had been travelling since we had left Vernag.

The bungalow at Hirpur was in the same style as the rest, but was unusually ruinous.

The veranda was tumbling down, there were big holes in the walls and the light shone through the roof. In this climate, however, there was very little objection to this unless it should chance to rain. The courtyard in which the bungalow is situated has a large ruined gateway which is evidently the remains of a handsome building. In fact, it was one of the old Mogul serais – short for caravanserais *(rest-houses)* – which were built by Jehangir and others of that ilk as rest-houses on their journeys to and from Cashmere, which was the favourite summer retreat of the Mogul Emperors. We found traces of these magnificent buildings after this, some in excellent preservation, at every stage of our journey to India.

Opposite the bungalow, on the other side of the enclosure, was another similar building, which we found full of calves. They were not at all afraid of us so I took the smallest up in my arms and carried him out to have his likeness taken. He did not object in any way, and kept his position quite nicely while I made my sketch. Soon afterwards he came up into the veranda, and I found him, with two friends of his own age and standing, in my bedroom, where they all seemed so suspiciously at home that I could not help suspecting that they lived there as much as in the building opposite. This was, in fact, almost as clean as, and in much better condition than, the so-called bungalow, and after exploring it we decided if it should rain seriously, to remove our things to the loft above the calves' abode which was quite watertight, whereas our roof was full of holes and our doors and windows were minus half their shutters. I think the villagers must have used some of them for firewood.

We could get no supplies at this place as the headman had locked up everything in the way of grain and gone away as soon as he heard of our approach. This is by no means a rare occurrence; the people in isolated villages seem to object to selling their grain and stores to travellers. Probably they only make a scanty provision for themselves as carriage is so difficult, and dislike having their stores reduced but, whatever the reason may be, we often had great difficulty in getting food for our servants. We had heard that it rained in these regions every day in the year, and we had scoffed at the idea, for when we arrived the weather was lovely. But, sure enough, in an hour or two the clouds began to gather on the neighbouring peaks, the thunder pealed from crag to crag, the wind rose, and we had a sharp shower of rain. As a natural consequence the temperature fell considerably. My husband was dressed in a Holland suit and I in a cotton dress, but directly the rain came we dived into our kiltas for various cloaks and wraps which we were thankful to put on. It is impossible to climb or travel at this time of the year here in warm clothes; still it is necessary to have something of the kind within reach.

Domestic animals in Cashmere are exceedingly tame - I have already mentioned the calves that came around us in the most confiding manner. While we were walking out in the evening to explore the valley we met a large flock of sheep and goats, which presently surrounded us. Being in their midst we stood still for them to pass, but they stopped and examined us with much curiosity. There were some very elegant silver-grey goats with long silky hair who licked our hands as we stroked them. This familiarity delighted us until one of the pretty creatures tore about a quarter of a yard of lace out of the sleeve of my dress and proceeded to eat it up, and another began devouring the tassels of a dressing gown in which, I regret to be obliged to state, my husband had arrayed himself for his evening walk.

Knowing that it would be cold when the sun went down, we had sent our coolies to gather some fir cones with which the ground was in many places strewn, so that we might have a fire at night. The coolies on this side of Cashmere speak neither Hindustani nor English, so that it is rather difficult to make them understand. In this case I sent Tom to fetch one of the biggest cones he could find, and this I showed to the coolies, spreading my arms abroad in a manner suggestive of any amount, and they understood at once and flew to do my bidding, returning with a fine collection.

When night came on we closed our windows and doors as near as might be, and proceeded to fill a niche in the wall, which represented a fireplace, with the cones. On a match being applied they blazed up in the most desirable manner, for they were full of turpentine, so we sat and warmed ourselves and enjoyed the blaze, feeding it now and then from the heap beside us. It was now that we found the benefit of the gaps in our doors and windows and the holes in the rafters, for though the smoke poured into the room it did not trouble us at all but found its way out as quickly as it came in.

Notwithstanding the state of the bungalow at Hirpur we certainly spent a very pleasant time there. The scenery around was so beautiful and the temperature such a delightful change from our late experiences, 'cool but not too cool' like old Mr. Woodhouse's gruel. The next day, knowing what a long stiff march was before us, we were in our saddles by half past five, having sent on the baggage ponies and coolies in charge of the bawarchi a couple of hours before. Too much had certainly not been said about the road. For a mile or so we went on gaily enough, and began to think it was not so bad after all, but then our troubles began. The ascents were never ending and fearful to look at; there was often no visible track and we hesitated which way to attempt. One hill in particular was very difficult. Recent rain had washed away all the stones and grass so that there was nothing on which the horses could get a foothold, and the poor creatures slipped terribly on the mud. I thought every moment we should have gone rolling to the bottom together, but my wise old horse managed to get up somehow. In many places it was quite impossible to ride and we had to dismount and scramble up or down as best we could. We had to cross water courses with the water rushing down them, the only way of proceeding with any speed being to choose the stones that were the least under water and to stay on them as short a time as possible - it was 'tripping the light fantastic toe' with a vengeance. At one place the rock had broken away considerably and curved inwards so that it was quite impossible to look over. A pathway is built over it, and it is artificially supported so that, except in rainy weather or darkness, the place is not absolutely dangerous, but the height of the precipice is very great, and the idea of a fall from it seemed unspeakably dreadful. It was in this very spot that, many years ago in the time of Aurungzebe, the hillside gave way under the weight of five elephants carrying the ladies of the emperor's seraglio *(harem)*, and they were all dashed to pieces below. I could quite imagine the catastrophe as I passed. There is also a legend about this place that goes back quite into the dark ages. An ogre called Lal Golam is said to have had his abode here, who killed travellers by throwing them over the precipice at this spot, and used afterwards to go down and eat them at his leisure.

The scenery throughout the whole of this march was most magnificent, far exceeding in grandeur anything we saw on the Murree route. The heights above and the depths below were something stupendous, and these mighty mountain passes were adorned with a profusion of wild flowers. Some of the slopes were perfectly blue with forget-me-nots, and ferns of the loveliest and rarest were everywhere in sweet confusion. Beside the ordinary English forget-me-not, there were some of a very dark blue, the eye in the centre being purple instead of yellow, and again there were others of a deep pink, almost crimson. There were lovely daphnes, primulas, and all sorts of flowers that we are accustomed to see in English hot-houses, some larger and coarser than their English sisters, and some perfect miniatures of them. The mountain air seems to give depth and richness to their colouring. I never saw such brilliant blues, such delicate peaches and lavenders, and such warm pinks and crimsons.

Aliabad Serai, whither we were bound, is three miles from the top of the pass, and turning the corner of a mountain we suddenly came in sight of it, a massive, square stone building on a grassy platform closely surrounded and overshadowed by enormous mountains. These are generally covered with snow, and I suppose there are only two or three months in the year when this is not the case. Just now they were truly 'in verdure clad', and such verdure - so fresh and vivid, as if it were living its short life with a fullness and intensity unknown to grass that has all the year to be green in. The serai, which is the only building in sight, is in good preservation. As we were dismounting beneath the fine arched gateway, we were accosted by a man who wanted us to give medicine to his son, and on our enquiring about the disease for which we were expected to treat him, a youth came forward with his arm hanging stiff and useless - he said it had been like that for more than a year. We had often administered simple medicines to the people in places where we had stopped. They seem to expect it of Europeans, and will take anything you give them most gratefully and confidingly. But this seemed a case beyond our very finite powers, so my husband had to inform the man that he was not a doctor and could do nothing for his son, whereupon they turned away sadly disappointed. It appeared to me that the lad's elbow had been dislocated, and nothing having been done to put it right, it was of course, useless.

This old rest-house of the Mogul Emperors is, as I have said, a square building, facing inwards looking into a courtyard, the only opening being the gateway that forms one side of the quadrangle. It is very massive and well built but the rooms, which are principally deep cavernous archways, have neither doors nor windows, and as it is situated in a gorge at a very high elevation and is exposed to bitter winds, warmth and shelter are most desirable even in summer. Notwithstanding the elaborate arrangements we made by hanging dhurries and waterproof sheets over the open doorways, we entirely failed to make the place in the least degree comfortable, and spent a miserable night with the wind whistling round our devoted heads. Still, our experiences were more cheerful than those of a friend of ours who told us that when he arrived at this place late one cold evening, thick snow was all around, a keen wind swept through the old stone building, and a man was dying of cholera in the courtyard, for whom he was called to prescribe. Now there is scarcely any snow to be seen, just a white streak here and there, and the mountains are covered with grass and flowers. Still, in spite of this, I never saw a more bleak, dreary-looking place, and this dreariness is, as it were, accentuated by the grave of an Englishman just on the edge of the plateau that overlooks the gorge. He was a doctor who had been to Cashmere during the cholera epidemic that raged there in 1876, and he died at this dismal, comfortless spot of cholera as he was on his way home. His grave has a plain slab with a cross on it, with his name and the date of his death. I cannot imagine anything more lonely than the spot that has been chosen. It was surrounded by the loveliest forget-me-nots and buttercups and all sorts of English flowers when we saw it, yet it makes me shiver to think what it must be like in winter, on this desolate wind-swept height, but –

'He feels no motion now, nor force,
He neither hears, nor sees,
Rolled round in one diurnal course
With rocks and stones and trees.'

We left Aliabad Serai at sunrise hoping, as the sky was cloudless, to get a good view of the Pass. We had about three miles to go, principally up a gentle ascent up a veritable flowery land, but once we had to cross a very rapid mountain torrent which looked as if it would carry the horses off their legs. Scarcely a tree was to be seen, but the opposite hills were covered with the whitened skeletons of what had been pine forests, the bark and branches of which had been taken by the hill men to feed their goats. They looked most melancholy - such wanton destruction shows the need of a Forestry Department.

Soon we reached the Pass of the Pir Panjal. Pir means holy man, and Panjal was, I suppose, the name of the particular Pir who is buried here. On the other side the ground seems, for a long way, to go down almost perpendicularly. The view was magnificent, but clouds came rolling up from beneath which, though very beautiful in themselves, were unwelcome as hiding what was immediately beneath us, but through a rift here and there we were able to catch a glimpse of the distant plains. We rested and looked our fill for about half an hour. At least I did, but Tom was very busy with an experiment in the boiling of an egg. He knew that an egg cannot be boiled hard on the top of Mont Blanc from the lessened pressure of the atmosphere and, though the Pir Panjal (11,600 feet) is not quite as high as Mont Blanc, he thought he should like to try what would be the effect at that elevation. The khansama had been charged accordingly to bring a kettle and an egg for the purpose. A fire was lighted, the kettle was presently boiling merrily and then the egg was placed in it. It was soon presented to us boiled hard - rather suspiciously soon, in fact, for it was scarcely heated through, and when the khansama was charged with having boiled if before he brought it, he meekly admitted the soft impeachment. It appeared that, like the Canterbury pilgrim who –

'That he might walk a little more at ease
Just took the liberty to boil his peas',

he had, before starting, taken the liberty to boil the egg thinking it was less likely to break on the road. So there is still a doubt whether an egg can be boiled hard on the Pir Panjal Pass.

The descent on the other side was terribly steep. It was impossible to ride and almost impossible to walk. How we did it I cannot imagine, for there is no pretence at a road; the narrow paths are broken away and are full of loose stones and shale that have been brought down by the melting snows. They were slippery with mud and however warily we walked we were continually slipping down a yard or two, stones and all. Now and then I was so tired that, notwithstanding the danger, and sorry as I was for my poor horse, I was really obliged to ride. After eight miles of this sort of travelling through the most grand and impressive scenery, we came to the rest house at Poshiana.

Now Poshiana is a most remarkable place, being simply a collection of flat-roofed huts clinging to the side of the mountain. Advantage is taken of a cavity, a roof of pine logs is laid across supported in front on pillars of pine wood, the roof is covered thickly with earth and the spaces between the pillars are filled up where considered necessary by plants or earth, and behold a house! A luxuriant crop of grasses generally grows on the roof which forms a favourite playground for the children and goats. The path over which we rode frequently passed over the roofs of these houses. I have seen babies playing on the very edge of them when the descent was sheer down the side of a precipice, which almost took away your breath to look at. The rest-house is simply one of these huts built into the mountainside. There was a door and a small hole in the wall for a window. There were some astonishing looking protuberances on the inside wall, which puzzled me but, on examination, they proved to be boulders of the mountain side protruding into the room, and the floor too was very uneven from the same cause.

This place, being closely surrounded by the huts of the villagers and being in other ways very unsatisfactory, we decided to push on to Baramgalla after a couple of hours' rest. It began to rain and the place and its surroundings were very dismal, so we started and in a few minutes were out of the cloud altogether and were able to dispense with our waterproofs and umbrellas. Our way now lay through a very deep and narrow valley – a gorge in fact – and was exceedingly rough and stony. There was no apparent path, and we had simply to climb over and round the boulders that strewed the way. Our horses showed themselves clever and willing at this sort of work but I found that, at the end of the day's journey, 'Greatheart', who had been shod only a few days before, had lost two of his shoes and broken a third.

A very turbulent stream ran through this valley and we had perforce to follow its windings, running continually close to the foot of the rocks on one side or the other. We had to cross it no less than twenty eight times. This was done by means of bridges which were all built of a couple of pine trunks laid across on irregular heaps of stones, roughly split logs laid across, tied with twigs and bits of bark. Our syce had occasionally to mend a bridge before we could go over. Where there was an unusually large hole he placed a stone on it, pressed some earth down round it, and signified to us that it was safe to cross. Bridge number sixteen was all on one side so that, in going over it, I felt as if I were crossing a sloping roof laterally. Number twenty-four was at an angle of forty-five degrees, being supported on a very high rock at one end, a small heap of stones at the other. I really felt great delicacy in attempting to cross this one, but my horse seemed to see nothing unusual in it, so over we went.

As we go on and the scenery grows in grandeur and beauty, the mountains are higher and closer together; as we climb their sides or meander through the valleys at their feet, we feel perfectly awestruck at the frowning height of the beetling crags above us. I was reminded of that line of somebody's on Byron –

'Black clouds his forehead bound, and at his feet were flowers',

for these majestic monsters were clothed with loveliness as with a garment; the vegetation was most exquisite and luxuriant, ferns, mosses, graceful trailing creepers, the rich and varied green of the foliage ending as one looked upward in the sombre darkness of the pines. All this, refreshed by daily rain and varied occasionally by a sparkling waterfall foaming and leaping down the mountainside, formed the perfection of mountain scenery.

CHAPTER 5

We reached Baramgalla at sunset after having been nearly ten hours in the saddle, doing twenty-one miles. The rest-house was strong and substantial, and very prettily situated. It had a floor of cement, which is the first one we have seen since we entered Cashmere - but we are now in the dominions of the Rajah of Poonch, a tributary of the Cashmere Maharaja. There were also a table and a few chairs which, added to our own, made us quite comfortable. As we had had six days' hard marching since we left Vernag, we therefore decided to remain two or three days in this place to rest and recoup, especially as the temperature was pleasant, and we knew that another march would take us into the heat again. 'Tis true there were no windows whatever, not even a hole in the wall, and when the doors were shut we were in utter darkness. This did not matter much, however, as we lived and had our meals in the veranda, only retiring to the inner room to sleep, and we had become so used to an airy out-of-door life that such things as windows and doors were of but little importance to us. I shall be very glad however to return to the trammels of civilization. For a time this wandering life is very fascinating and the shifts to which we are put cause us much amusement, but that sort of joke soon palls upon a cultivated taste, and ceases to be funny. Therefore, although the plains of India are by no means alluring in August and September, my heart grew light at the thought of getting back to all my 'little comforts', and to the repose, cleanliness and abundance which I always accepted as a matter of course, and scarcely valued till now.

We stayed three nights and two days at Baramgalla. It rained most of the time so we sat in the veranda and read, or wrote letters, now and then wandering out between the showers to gather flowers and ferns. Once we found some mushrooms, which we carried home to give a flavour to the inevitable morghi. I certainly ate them with some trepidation but no ill consequences resulted. Mutton is now an unattainable luxury; we have not been able to get any since we left Vernag. While at Baramgalla we got very much at sea with regard to the time, Tom having forgotten to wind up his watch and the weather being so cloudy and rainy that there was no sign of the sun. For instance, one day we called for dinner and ate it, at what we thought about sunset, but to our great bewilderment it continued to be light for some three hours, and we had time to get very hungry again before bedtime.

Having noticed that the rain rarely set in heavily before noon, we resolved to make an early start. We accordingly rose and dressed by candlelight, but did not get off earlier than usual after all, as there was a good deal of difficulty in loading the coolies and baggage animals. The men here, although they are paid half as much again as coolies in other parts of Cashmere, have no arrangements for fastening their loads, and as they carry their burden awkwardly on their heads and shoulders, instead of on their backs, they can only take a very small amount, and are very troublesome and unruly. From the beginning of our travels, we had entrusted to our khansama all arrangements relating to our baggage. If ever the coolies appealed to us, we referred them back to him, as if we were far superior to such vulgar cares. This plan answered admirably, for the unquestioned authority which he enjoyed gave him great prestige among them. They always addressed him as 'Huzoor' – *Your Honour* – or 'Gureeb Pawar' – *Preserver of the Poor*; this fully repaid him for any extra trouble he had in the matter, and he seemed to take pride in spending as little money as possible.

The road from Baramgalla to Thana Mandi was worse than any we had travelled, and unfortunately Tom elected to walk it. We knew we had to cross the Rattan Pir Range, but as we were already at a considerable elevation we thought we had only to go a little higher, and that then it would be all downhill. But alas, we had to go five miles uphill and then five miles down; the path was often ankle deep in slippery mud and sometimes it was merely a watercourse, over the stony bottom of which we had to go splashing and stumbling as best we could. Where the stones were firm we could get over the ground with comparative ease, but unfortunately they were generally loose stones, evidently lately brought down by the rains, and they rolled in all directions beneath our feet. It would have been a stiff march under any circumstances, but going over it as we did in the rains, it was very difficult, and though I could now and then ride and rest myself, poor Tom had to trudge the whole ten miles.

We had some splendid views, though, on our way, different in character from anything we had seen before. The view from the top of the Rattan Pir is very extensive and, I think, far finer than that from the Pir Panjal itself. After crossing the mountain we plunged into clouds, and for a time could see only a few yards before us. It is easy to understand why there is so much rain on the tops of these mountains; from every gully or pass the warm vapour is continually streaming up from the plains towards the heights where the cooler air turns it speedily into rain. To all the plants we have seen I must now add the holly, and there was also a great deal of clematis today, climbing over the bushes. We also saw some lungoors, or big grey-faced monkeys, in the depths of the forest. They were chattering and pulling down branches as we passed. We seldom see animals of any kind and as the only spots inhabited by man are the stages where we rest, the silence of our journeys is only broken by the sound of our own footsteps and the noise of rushing waters.

Thana Mandi is at the very foot of the Rattan Pir. The rest house looks imposing and has a fine raised veranda overlooking the valley; the whole place however, was extremely neglected and dirty. Nothing was fit to touch, and necessity alone induced us to remain. On opening one of the doors the first thing that greeted our eyes was an enormous scorpion, the largest we had ever seen. Tom tried to kill it with an alpenstock, but it took refuge in a hole in the wall and, though he nearly knocked the house down in his efforts to get at it, he only succeeded in killing a young one, doubtless a relative, so the creature remained at large somewhere about our bedroom and we had visions of it all the time we were there.

Thana Mandi is also in the Poonch territory, and as we had heard that the Rajah had a separate issue of stamps, and knew that they must be very rare, we wanted to get some for our children in England. There were none at Baramgalla, the tekadar explaining by saying that the people there did not often write letters. Tom therefore wrote to the Rajah of Poonch asking for some of his stamps, and sent a coolie with the letter and some money. When we left Baramgalla this coolie had not yet returned, and we almost despaired of our Poonch stamps but, while we were sitting in the veranda at Thana Mandi, he suddenly appeared before us and informed us pathetically that he was dead from the hardships of the journey. We told him to sit down while we examined the letter he had brought, and finding that it had contained the desired rarities we gave him a reward which brought him to life and sent him on his way rejoicing.

It rained nearly all day, so we simply rested, and ate, and then slept, and were in our saddles before sunrise, on our way to Rajaori, a fourteen mile march. On leaving the bungalow at Thana Mandi we had to pass the ruins of a fine old Mogul serai; the gateway was still very fine and many of the rooms in the quadrangle in good repair, for the Mogul Emperors did not build for a year, or a week, or a day, but had some idea of perpetuating their memories.

Directly the sun rose above the hilltops we found it very hot. The road was still exceedingly rough, though not so steep as it had been. It seems that when the rain comes down the mountains it naturally chooses the roads as convenient channels and, as nothing whatever is done to turn it aside, they become mere watercourses. All the earth is washed away from them, nothing being left but big loose stones which seem as if they had all been collected and thrown there, and over which it is most difficult and trying to have to march for miles, the sole variety being that sometimes they are dry and sometimes under water.

We reached Rajaori exhausted by the heat, which reminded us painfully that we were returning to India in the middle of the hot season. The rest-house there is a pleasure palace of the old Moguls; it is built on the banks of the river Tavi opposite to the town, which looks most delightfully picturesque and mediaeval on the other side. We passed first through a shady but utterly neglected garden in which we could still perceive traces of arbours and fountains, and finally bestowed ourselves and our possessions in the old pavilion. There are two sets of rooms facing inwards, and between these is a large open space with its roof supported on pillars. From this there is a pretty view of the river and the town. The place is very old and there are flights of steps leading up to the terraced roof, and down into dark dungeon-like places underground. As I was peering down one of these stairways, something dark and sinister disappeared round the corner. No doubt it was the wing of a bat, but it had all the effect of the fragment of the ghost of an old Mogul escaping from my intrusive curiosity and plunging into the darkness.

We slept in the open pavilion for the sake of the current of air. The river murmured immediately below us, and the fireflies – another reminder of India – flitted in and out. The atmosphere of the place was very eerie - the dark archways and the yawning look of the empty rooms made me feel as if, at any moment, an Old Mogul might appear and address himself to us. We were disturbed however, by something more substantial - a terrific thunderstorm arose. The noise was deafening, and the lightning seemed to play round us in the most lively fashion. In the morning the river, which on the previous day had crawled along unimpressively between banks of dry stones, had swollen to four times its size and was tearing along like a raging maniac.

The ford being opposite our windows, we had amused ourselves the day before by watching people crossing. Now it was our own khansama, with his clothes considerably tucked up and his coat folded in a bundle on his head, conducted by the dhobie *(washerman/washerwoman)* who, being a resident of the place was doing the honours of

Rajaori

the ford with the air of an habitué; now it was a fat old gentleman on horseback, with a white umbrella, who ambled gaily over. But after the storm, crossing the Tavi was a serious matter. The ford was quite impassable and soon even the strongest swimmers had to wait till the violence of the current had somewhat subsided. I could quite understand how it was that, in an excess of turbulent fury like the present, it had washed away two enormous stone piers of a bridge which the Rajah was building over it, and which still stands unfinished, a monument of the river's great strength. We were interested in its changed appearance knowing that we should have to cross it that same afternoon.

We sent off our servants and coolies at eleven so that they might get well ahead of us and be at Changas Serai, our next stage fifteen miles off, ready to receive us. We ourselves did not start till two, and after having gone about half a mile, upon coming to the place where we had to cross the river, we were more surprised than pleased to see items of our baggage strewn about the ground, and to recognize the dishevelled forms of our cook and khansama gesticulating on the distant shore. It turned out that, on reaching the ford, the coolies had all thrown down their loads and declared themselves unable to carry them over, as the flood was so deep and strong. After a time, as it abated, two men more daring than the rest were induced by large promises on the part of the khansama to go backwards and forwards transporting each package separately on their heads. This accounted for the delay, for the mules and ponies had to be all unloaded, as the water would have been over the backs of some of them and, heavily laden as they were, they could not have kept their footing. My trusty old steed took me across safely with a man swimming and wading on each side of him. There were terrible moments when he seemed to be taken quite off his legs, and agonizing thrills went through me when he stumbled into a hole. Though I tucked up my feet in the most extraordinary and ingenious manner, it was impossible to help getting wet, but presently I was safe on dry land again, welcomed with delighted exclamations of praise and thanksgiving from the servants who had watched the transit with great anxiety as also had my husband from the further shore. He, having seen that it was safe to cross, now began to make animated gestures, which I at last made out to mean that I was to send my horse back for him. Unfortunately, on this occasion he had an even smaller and weaker pony than usual - it would have been quite impossible for him to go over the river on it. So back went my poor horse and I had the very doubtful amusement of watching Tom's progress across the roaring flood. He was not half as clever in gathering himself up as I was, and his legs simply dragged through the water the whole way. Presently he too was welcomed with enthusiastic demonstrations and, leaving the servants to finish the transit and follow, we proceeded on our way.

But first Tom's pony distinguished himself by having a good roll in the mud before anyone could prevent him, so having regard to his frightfully dirty condition, as well as his weak-kneedness and incapacity generally, Tom determined to exchange him for a tall strong-looking mule that was among the baggage animals. He had never ridden a mule, and thought he should like to add this to his other experiences, and from this time forward he provided me with a series of entertainments which enlivened the way so much that the march, though longer than that of the day before, seemed much less tedious. When we came to a tiny rill, a few inches wide, across the path, this mule refused it in the most determined manner. His personal attendant did his utmost by dragging at him in front, and his justly incensed rider brought his influence to bear by whacking him behind, but no! he bore it all, and looked as if he would bear anything rather than risk his neck at such a formidable torrent. At last, Tom had to dismount, and the man took the mule to another place and, with much coaxing and many threats, at length dragged him over. Soon after this, as we were going down a very steep hill, I heard fresh shouts and objurgations - the saddle had slipped over his neck and hung there like a necklace, he being a tall, sloping animal with no shoulders to speak of, so the saddle had not much hold on him.

After a great deal of arrangement, we started again but in a short time I heard a great scuttering behind me, and turning quickly saw the mule go down over the side of the path and my husband sprawling on the ground. I was rather frightened at this, but the mule did not fall far, and began to eat grass while still on the ground. Tom rose ruefully, saying with a sardonic smile that he would never trust a 'sure-footed mule' again. We arranged ourselves once more, resolving to proceed slowly and carefully and hoping to meet with no more catastrophes, but alas, in a little while, the saddle was hanging round the mule's neck again, so Tom got off and decided that it would be pleasanter and less trouble to walk than to go on bestriding such an exceedingly uncomfortable animal merely for the honour and glory of the thing. In going up and down these steep hills the strain on the saddle and girths is very great, and it is necessary to have a crupper as well as a strong leather strap round the horse's chest. I have both and find them very useful.

We saw a great many cactuses on this march; our way was often bordered by thick hedges of them and sometimes they had grown into quite large trees. We had another reminder of India, too, in the shape of a palm tree standing quite alone on the mountainside. It looked very strange in its 'solitary grace', and I wondered how it came there.

Just before reaching Changas Serai we passed the ruins of a fine Mogul serai, built in the usual style of solid magnificence. Some of the columns had given way, and the tops of the arches had fallen down and lay upon the ground in huge masses. With a very little trouble and expense many of these monuments of India's past greatness might be put, and kept, in repair and rendered habitable. But they are, on the contrary, completely given up to ruin and decay, while the Maharaja builds on their very thresholds - as if to mark the contrast - houses, the slovenly workmanship and clumsy construction of which render them only fit for cattle sheds. The waste of power and material in this country is enormous. No building is ever repaired or kept up, time and the climate are allowed to do their work, the roof falls through, the pillars crumble away, the doors drop off their hinges and, when the place is finally uninhabitable, another like unto it is built, and the ruin is left standing, the old materials, even, not being made use of.

These bungalows are littered with old broken furniture - chairs without legs or arms and with broken backs and seats, tables that can no longer stand alone, and dirty tattered beds, the very look of which take away all thought of repose. A little timely attention would have kept these things useful and respectable, but the 'stitch in time' is an idea which has not yet penetrated into Cashmere.

The resthouse at Changas Serai is on the edge of a hill about two hundred feet above the Tavi. The heat was stifling so we had chairs placed outside and sat overlooking the river till darkness came on, but still no servants had arrived. At last, they began to straggle in by degrees, and we ventured to rejoice; but alas, the coolie with the lantern was far behind, and it was past ten o' clock before we got a light and something to eat. We had our beds placed in the veranda but could not get a breath of air till at last, to our great relief, a heavy storm broke. This effectually prevented our getting off at four a.m., as we had intended, and we could not start till seven, but it had cooled and cleared the air and we had consequently a pleasant shady march, winding along over mountains that overlook the valley of the Tavi.

Now this Tavi is an ugly river; when quiet it is sullen and insignificant, and when roused it is turgid and tumultuous. From the nature of the soil through which it passes, it is of a dull, dirty red colour and reminded me of an ugly red-faced man in a passion, and the antipodes of the gay, graceful, delicate Sind. During the march we had twice to cross swollen streams, which was a work of some anxiety, but on this occasion Tom had a pony of respectable height, and so was able to keep his feet out of the water. The valley was open and the views both before and behind us were very beautiful, but the vegetation was no longer so luxuriant as it had been. In fact, it was often somewhat scanty, and the hills were much disfigured by the marks of forest fires. As it was a cloudy day, the lights and shadows, which form the great beauty of the scenery, were wanting, but these we were quite willing to forego in consideration of being able to ride along in comparative coolness.

We often passed skeletons of animals by the wayside; horses and buffaloes, but more often they were camels, which had probably got hurt in passing over these terrible roads and had then been left to die by the wayside. They looked very melancholy, but more melancholy than all was the form of a dying bullock by the wayside. It was in the last stage of emaciation and we thought it dead till, just as we passed, it horrified us by giving a convulsive kick and rolling its dying eyes. These people are as averse to killing a bullock to shorten its last agonies as we are to killing a man for the same reason, and it sometimes seems that our prejudice is as unreasonable as theirs. Still, on the whole man individually is not to be trusted with the fate of his fellows; the final blow should be struck by some power above and beyond him, not liable to be influenced by his paltry and interested motives.

The town of Naushera lies in the middle of an extensive plain; it could be seen for some two or three miles as we wound along the hillside, descending by degrees, and formed quite a picturesque object. As usual, the ruins of the Mogul serai were very fine and very prominent; the castellated walls, and massive towers and bastions were on a grander scale than usual, and looked most imposing. There is also a very handsome Hindoo temple, evidently lately built and painfully new which, as to details and finish, was the finest we had seen in Cashmere. The town itself is merely a collection of the ordinary dirty, rickety houses and a few shops. The rest-house was as dirty and dilapidated as any we have seen, though about twenty yards from it stands the substantial and well-built ruin of another bungalow which was shaken by an earthquake some years ago - a very little outlay, a quarter of what was spent on the new one, would have put it into good repair again. Just outside the veranda, under some trees, is the grave of a little English child who died here some eight years ago, while its parents were travelling. The wooden cross that marks the grave is very much eaten by white ants, but the inscription can easily be read, and the rough stone wall that surrounds it is intact. It was very sad for the parents to have to leave their little one here; it certainly enhances our grief when we have to lay our dead to rest and leave them under alien skies, and Tennyson expresses a very natural yearning when he says –

''Tis well, 'tis something, we may stand
Where he in English earth is laid,
And from his ashes may be made
The violet of his native land'.

Both the house and the veranda being frightfully stuffy, we decided to sleep outside under the trees, but this arrangement was not altogether a success. To begin with the mosquitoes were very troublesome, and before we had been able to forget these, the horses which were grazing near us appeared to be suddenly struck with our unusual appearance and to regard us as something supernatural. As their legs were tied together to prevent their straying, their struggles to get out of the neighbourhood of the supposed horrors were very noisy and energetic. A little later our slumbers were disturbed by heavy rain falling, which made us bestir ourselves speedily, and we had soon lighted the lantern and dragged our beds into the shelter of the veranda, taking especial care to collect all our clothes which had been hung out to air. Again we composed to sleep but in an hour or so a great cry arose from the unfortunate Tom who had just awakened and found to his dismay that his favourite boots had been left outside and were half full of water. He seemed to have no scruple in arousing the whole establishment to inform them of the fact! I sympathised as much as could be expected of me, considering that they were not actually my boots, and was, after a time, permitted to resume my interrupted slumbers.

As the rain continued we were not able to start in the morning and when, after a time, it ceased the servants brought word that a stream a short distance from the house had risen to such an extent that it was impossible to cross it except by swimming. We went to look at it and saw people crossing by holding on to mussacks, or inflated skins; they were carried a good way down the stream, but still they got over safely. However, no luggage could be carried in this way, so we had to wait several hours while the water went down, the servants from time to time bringing us word of its progress. At last it was safe for us to cross, so we started on our march to Saidabad. Tom had his choice today between riding a pony with a young foal dangling at its heels, or a small mule which I thought – even for a mule – looked exceedingly like a donkey, though of course I had too much delicacy of feelings to say so when I found that he decided upon riding it. Being wishful to avoid the difficulties he had experienced with the previous mule, he ordered the man to bring the saddle and bridle to which the animal had been accustomed and which were likely to fit it. The saddle was a structure built of wood with a ridge behind and a pinnacle in front, profusely ornamented with brass nails. It had a drapery on each side trimmed with a red and green fringe, and the crupper was of stamped leather ornamented with blue beads. In startling contrast to all this splendour was the bridle, which was of unalleviated rope; the stirrup 'leathers' were also of rope and were of different lengths. Tom mounted, however, and rode on sadly, and when I presently questioned him as to the cause of his silence and depression, he confessed that he couldn't help thinking about the death of William the Conqueror and, on observing the extraordinary construction of his saddle in front, I could not fail to understand the historical allusion, and thought he had real cause for anxiety!

We resolved to travel slowly so that the servants might not lag behind and keep us waiting till nearly midnight for our dinner, as they did at Changas Serai. We therefore dismounted now and then and let our horses graze, while we sat in the shade and ate gingerbread till the coolies had passed us, and if ever they got behind we waited again and thus kept them well ahead till the last. This was our last march but one. We had now come nearly to the end of our tour, and our greatest hardship was the want of bread. We little thought when we had it every day that the deprivation of it would be felt so severely. We had by this time finished all our biscuits too, and the only thing of the kind that remained to us was a tin of gingerbread which, though excellent in its way, did not go well with Bologna sausages, sardines or bacon, which was all we had left. We had not been able to get butter or vegetables or meat of any kind for many days, and the marches were so difficult and exhausting that we had not the heart to make our servants do anything except what was absolutely necessary, so that we really suffered great privations. The heat too was most trying and we had generally to march in the middle of the day, owing to the swollen state of the streams in the early morning. Every day we hoped for an easier march and better roads, but each journey seemed more toilsome than the last. We should not have minded the heat and weariness so much, if we could have looked forward to a comfortable room and a good meal at the end of it, but we knew that after all our toil and travail only a bare shelter awaited us. And when our poor tired servants had arranged our scanty belongings in the least musty and frowsy corner of the dirty neglected bungalow, and had hurriedly prepared a meal from our scanty stores, we sat down to eat it, meekly and thankfully it is true, but without much relish or satisfaction. This makes all the difference between Asiatic and European travelling.

There are four ranges of mountains between Cashmere and the Indian plains: the Pir Panjal, the Rattan Pir, the Kaman Gosha - which we crossed on this march from Naushera to Saidabad - and the Aditak, which latter range seems to rise sheer from the plains. The Kaman Gosha is the least steep of the four, but the road over it is long and rough, though sometimes the scenery is very pretty. We often passed the dead bodies of animals, and were generally apprised of their whereabouts before we saw them by the incredible effluvium that hung about in their neighbourhood. Any creature that dies seems to be left where it lies to poison the surrounding atmosphere till the beasts of the field and the fowls of the air have performed the last kind offices upon its carcass.

We passed also several graves that looked as if jackals or other wild beasts had been at them. There seem to be no regular burying grounds in this country, but the people just bury their dead here and there in small groups, with heaps of stones piled over them in an oblong form. Sometimes flowers are growing among the stones – principally irises - but there is no monument or inscription. On this march we saw several palms, but not very fine ones; they looked rather miserable, as if not quite at home.

The legend of Bluebeard must have had its rise in this part of the world for on this march we constantly met men with their long beards dyed of a deep indigo blue. I have often, both here and in India, seen men with hair and beards dyed red, but here blue beards seem to be the fashion, though the men who wear them are not dandies in any other respect and could scarcely be suspected of vanity with regard to their personal appearance, their whole costume consisting of a dingy loin cloth and a dirty whitey-brown turban. The grey wollen garment, I am glad to say, disappeared directly we came to the warmer side of the pass.

As we approached Saidabad we saw, crowning one of the hills on the opposite side of the valley, a most imposing looking fort. It was glorified by the setting sun, and from its commanding position looked really magnificent. It was built, I find, by Ranjeet Singh, the Lion of the Punjab, and is now occupied by the Maharaja's police. We reached Saidabad at sunset and speedily arranged ourselves to the best advantage in the squalid dingy bungalow, resolving to start as early in the morning as possible. My husband accordingly roused up the servants at 2 a.m. with orders to send off the luggage. Upon waking a few hours later, and finding it was raining heavily, he was much relieved to find that his orders had not been carried out, and we were presently informed that we should not be able to start till the afternoon as there were several streams on our road to Bhimber that would be very deep and rapid after the rain.

We composed ourselves, therefore, to write letters all the morning and started on our last march at about 2 p.m. Just before we left, an old man came detailing various familiar symptoms, and asking for medicine. Tom, who has a most unnatural pleasure in seeing other people take medicine, willingly prescribed for him, and it was really most entertaining to see the old gentleman's smiling face as he leisurely munched two or three pills, and then placidly swallowed a stimulating and comforting concoction composed of nearly all the medicines in our possession. He was very grateful, but perhaps it was as well that we left before consequences ensued, although Tom has no doubt in his own mind that the old man was permanently benefitted by his prescriptions.

The journey to Bhimber was about fifteen miles. It was frightfully hot and the road very difficult and toilsome as it is entirely unmade throughout and is encumbered with huge boulders. We had to do a great deal of severe climbing and my brave old horse was so overcome by the steepness of the way and the heat combined that I feared he would 'burst his mighty heart'. I had to dismount and let him rest over and over again, and resolved then and there to send him back at once from Bhimber, and to take the tonga from thence to Gujrat.

When we had crossed the Aditak Range and were on the southern side of the mountains, the plains lay spread before us like a map. How well we knew the straight line of the far off horizon, and the yellow hazy look of the intervening flat expanse, simmering as it were in the broiling heat of the July sun. With heavy hearts we began to make our last descent. The way was rough and broken; much soil had been dislodged by the recent rains. In some places there had been considerable landslips and the road looked most dangerous. The mountains, which were made of sandstone, had not the look of stability which generally marks a mountainous country, and which doubtless gave rise to the phrase – 'the everlasting hills'. They gave the impression of having only recently been run up, and looked as if they were already crumbling to pieces. The soil was dry and arid and the vegetation stunted and scanty. A verdant spot in the vast yellow plain beneath us was pointed out to us as Bhimber, so we took courage and plodded along thinking our journey was nearly at an end, but alas, when we had reached the foot of the mountains, eight weary miles still lay before us.

Wide turbulent streams came in our way at every turn, on the banks of any one of which I should have sat down in utter despair of crossing a month ago, but at whose appearance I now only felt annoyance and weariness. One river in particular we had to cross five times for want of blowing up a rock and making a few yards of road here and there. By the time we had reached Bhimber we had crossed nine streams of from 30 to 50 yards wide. At the last one I was tired to death and could scarcely sit on my horse. The poor beast was much exhausted and found it difficult to keep his legs against the violence of the current. I could feel him swaying under me and my husband, who was on the shore waiting for the horse to be sent back for him, saw me fix my eyes with melancholy desperation on a certain rock standing out of the stream, evidently deciding to direct my course to it and to cling there should I be carried away by the current as I momentarily expected. We got over somehow, but I was almost past caring what happened, and while in this state of mental and physical dejection we met a traveller who had just started on his first march from Bhimber. His dress and appearance were immaculate, his luggage and belongings all spick and span and new, and the contrast which he presented to us with our weather-beaten appearance and dilapidated travel-stained baggage was quite painful. 'How nice and neat he looks', exclaimed I, in envious admiration. 'So did the Prodigal Son' replied my husband 'when he **set out** on his journey'. Whereupon I laughed, and felt comforted with the thought of the different appearance the traveller would probably present at the end of his tour.